MW01234257

A Play in Three Acts

REBEL WITHOUT A CAUSE

Dramatized by
JAMES FULLER

Based upon the motion picture
"Rebel Without a Cause"

Dramatic Publishing
Woodstock, Illinois • London, England • Melbourne, Australia

Rebel without a Cause

A Play in Three Acts

FOR THIRTEEN MEN, TEN WOMEN AND EXTRAS*

CHARACTERS

A MAN......................................*a passer-by*
BUZZ GUNDERSON...................*a "wheel" in school*
JIM STARK........................*a new boy in school*
OFFICER MULLEN.....................*a police sergeant*
JUDY BROWN........................*the girl Jim likes*
PLATO...............................*Jim's new friend*
MRS. DAVIS.........................*a friend to Plato*
RAY..............................*a juvenile officer*
MR. STARK ⎫
MRS. STARK ⎰ ....*Jim's parents*
GRANDMA.........................*Mr. Stark's mother*
BELLE..........................*Judy's younger sister*
MISS HANNINGTON................*a high school teacher*
CRUNCH ⎫
GOON |
MOOSE ⎬ ....*the gang*
HELEN |
MILLIE ⎭
LECTURER ....*at planetarium*
MR. BROWN ⎫
MRS. BROWN ⎰ ....*Judy's parents*
OFFICER ONE
OFFICER TWO
EXTRAS, *if desired*....STUDENTS, POLICE OFFICERS, CROWD,
where indicated

---

*Several of these roles may be played by the same actors. See Notes on Characters and Costumes.

PLACE: *Any fair-sized American city.*
TIME: *The present.*

SYNOPSIS

ACT ONE: *Evening, and the following day.*
ACT TWO: *Evening of the same day.*
ACT THREE: *Still later the same evening.*

NOTES ON CHARACTERS
AND COSTUMES

. BUZZ: He is about eighteen, and combines an attractive nature with a desperate need to prove himself the most fearless and strongest man in his world. He is liked, feared and admired by the gang. He wears levis or blue jeans, a dark solid-color sport shirt, a leather jacket and boots.

JIM: Jim is seventeen and wears glasses part of the time. He is trying to please his parents and at the same time fighting a desperate battle to avoid being like them. When he isn't fighting this battle he is a warm, friendly person. In the first scene he wears a suit, and his necktie is loose. Later in Act One he wears a shirt and tie, slacks, and a jacket of a very distinctive cut and color. He wears these same clothes for the remainder of the play.

GANG: The members of the gang are all in their teens. The boys wear suede coats or leather jackets, tight levi pants or blue jeans, sport shirts, and boots. The girls wear dark skirts, plain boyish blouses, and suit jackets, cardigans or leather jackets. The clothing of the gang is not uniform, but the air they assume is uniform—swaggering, self-conscious, tyrannical.

OFFICER MULLEN: He can be any age, and has learned to take his job in its stride. He is not cynical, just practical. He is in his shirt sleeves throughout, and wears dark trousers, a white shirt, and a dark tie.

JUDY: Judy is sixteen and quite attractive, for which she compensates by being sullen and indifferent. She wears a good-looking dress, high heels, and a little too much make-up on her first appearance. Later she changes to simple school clothes, which she wears for the rest of the play. She carries a sweater during the scene of the chicken-run in Act Two.

PLATO: He is fifteen, a dark, rather handsome lad, but lonely-looking. He is small for his age. He wears slacks and a sport shirt upon his first appearance. Later he may add a jacket or sport coat.

MRS. DAVIS: She is a middle-aged, dignified colored lady. She wears a plain dress and hat.

RAY: Ray is fairly young, a soft-spoken, sympathetic juvenile officer. He wears a plain suit, and a hat at times.

MOTHER [Mrs. Stark]: She is middle-aged, a chic but rather hard-faced woman. She is well-dressed in party clothes upon her first appearance. Later in Act One she appears in a house-coat. In Act Two she first appears in a simple dress. Later she changes to an attractive housecoat and nightgown. In Act Three she wears a dress and a light coat.

FATHER [Mr. Stark]: He is a middle-aged man who has tried to please his family by being loving and generous, not because of real strength but rather because he is so terribly afraid of being rejected and unloved if he ever tries to assert himself. His family treats him half contemptuously. He may wear a tux in his first scene. Later in the act he changes to a business suit. During Act Two he takes off his suit coat and dons a woman's apron. He wears his suit again in Act Three, and a hat.

GRANDMA: She is small, in her sixties, chic and bright-eyed, and determined to stay young. She, too, wears party clothes in Act One, later changing to a simple house dress, her hair up in curlers.

MISS HANNINGTON: She is a schoolteacher in her early thirties, with no illusions about the present generation of school children. She wears a simple dress or suit and a hat.

LECTURER: This part should be played by a person with a good speaking voice. The manner is quiet but forceful, indicating a genuine feeling for the work.

BELLE: Belle is fourteen, and uncomplicated as yet. She wears school clothes.

MR. BROWN: Mr. Brown is in his early forties, a pleasant but unimaginative man who is baffled because Judy is now grown up and he doesn't quite know how to treat her. He means well but lacks understanding. He wears a business suit.

MRS. BROWN: She is about the same age as her husband, comfortable, warm-hearted and a good mother, but she, too, lacks the ability to get close to Judy. She wears a simple house dress.

EXTRAS: The Police Officers wear uniforms. The extra students wear school clothes, while spectators, if used in Act Three, wear everyday clothes.

NOTE: If you wish to use fewer men, two actors can handle five of the male parts: The Man, Officer Mullen, and Officer Number One can be handled by one actor, and Mr. Brown and Officer Number Two by another. Several of the female roles may also be played by one actress: Mrs. Brown and the Lecturer can be played by one person, and Miss Hannington and Grandma by another actress.

CHART OF STAGE POSITIONS

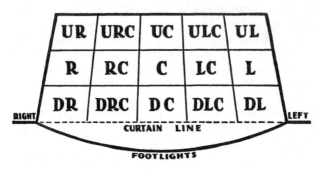

STAGE POSITIONS

Upstage means away from the footlights, *downstage* means toward the footlights, and *right* and *left* are used with reference to the actor as he faces the audience. R means *right*, L means *left*, U means *up*, D means *down*, C means *center*, and these abbreviations are used in combination, as: U R for *up right*, R C for *right center*, D L C for *down left center*, etc. One will note that a position designated on the stage refers to a general territory, rather than to a given point.

NOTE: Before starting rehearsals, chalk off your stage or rehearsal space as indicated above in the *Chart of Stage Positions*. Then teach your actors the meanings and positions of these fundamental terms of stage movement by having them walk from one position to another until they are familiar with them. The use of these abbreviated terms in directing the play saves time, speeds up rehearsals, and reduces the amount of explanation the director has to give to his actors.

PROPERTIES

GENERAL: Police Station: bench; desk (or table) and chair; two straight chairs; on desk, pad and pencil, telephone, papers and forms. Dining-room in Jim's home: table and four chairs; table set for four for breakfast, with glass of milk in front of Jim's place, orange juice and coffee only for Mother; morning mail; morning paper. Planetarium: several rows of straight chairs (folding type); small podium; knife for one of gang to toss to Jim. Dining-room in Judy's home: table set for four for dinner (including glasses of tomato juice). Another room in Jim's home: couch; small end table with lamp and alarm clock; easy chair; Jim's shoes under couch, his jacket over back of easy chair; piece of paper and pencil in drawer of end table. Old blanket U R C (Act Three); stretcher and blanket offstage (Act Three).

BUZZ: Match, knife, hamburger.

MAN: Several packages (one containing a wind-up toy), pack of cigarettes.

JUDY: Schoolbooks, hamburger.

MOTHER: Brown paper bag supposedly containing a lunch, handkerchief.

RAY: Pen, cigarettes and matches, portable microphone.

FATHER: Three cigars, two plates of eggs, wallet with two dollar bills.

GRANDMA: Plate of toast.

PLATO: Length of tire chain, handkerchief, gun.*

BELLE: Pitcher of milk, dish (supposedly a soufflè).

MRS. BROWN: Two covered vegetable dishes.

JIM: Flashlight lantern, rouge (in pocket) to smear on his shirt to simulate blood (end of Act One).

CRUNCH: Flashlight.

GOON: Flashlight, length of tire chain.*

MOOSE: Flashlight.

OFFICER ONE *and* OFFICER TWO: Guns.

STUDENTS: Some may carry schoolbooks.

* See Production Notes at back of playbook.

ACT ONE

[*The play is staged against a curtain backdrop in three playing areas located at the right side of the stage, in the center, and at the left side of the stage. Ideally, the space stage technique should be used, which consists of lighting, with spotlights only, the playing areas actually in use and leaving the rest of the stage in darkness. However, the play can be staged with great effectiveness with the whole stage lit at all times except between scenes. In the main, furniture and properties are a few chairs and tables. They are representational in nature and not important to the action of the play.*]

AT RISE OF CURTAIN: *It is evening. The* C *area is lit. The rest of the stage is in darkness. After a moment, whistling is heard offstage* L. *The whistling moves toward the stage, and as the figure approaches the light, we see a* MAN *walking briskly and cheerfully, carrying some packages. As he approaches the left end of the lighted area,* BUZZ *steps into the extreme edge of the up right portion of the lighted area and speaks in a friendly, cool voice.*]

BUZZ. That was pretty what you were whistling. Whistle some more. [MAN *stops nervously, whistles a nervous phrase, and tries to make a joke of a situation which he doesn't understand.* BUZZ *interrupts suddenly.*] You got a cigarette?

[*While this goes on, figures begin to crowd in from* D R *stage, gathering in a semi-circle around* BUZZ *and the* MAN. *They are boys and girls, all quite young. The boys wear suede coats or leather jackets, black levi pants, boots, and sport shirts. The girls wear dark skirts, plain boyish blouses, and suit jackets, cardigans, or leather jackets. Their clothing is*

*not uniform. It is the air they assume which is uniform—
swaggering, self-conscious, tyrannical.*]

MAN [*replying to* BUZZ]. Oh, I think so. [*Fumbles in his
pocket, finds a pack of cigarettes, brings it out, and drops it
in his nervousness. The figures wait while he picks it up and
offers one to* BUZZ, *holding them out.*] Filter tips.

BUZZ [*smiling, encouragingly*]. You smoke it. Smoke it, Dad.
[MAN *looks around the group, halfway starts to offer cigarettes to other people in group, who are now slowly closing
about him.* BUZZ *continues pleasantly but at same time men-
acingly.*] Go ahead, Dad, smoke it—like I told you. [*Lights
a match and holds it for* MAN.] I'll light it for you, Dad.
[*As* MAN *leans forward,* BUZZ *suddenly hits him.* MAN
*grunts, drops packages, and turns to run as figures close
around him.* BUZZ *continues to hit the now almost invisible*
MAN, *who shrieks and breaks away, is caught, struck again,
breaks away, and runs out* D L, *closely pursued by everyone
on stage. During this, not a word is spoken or a cry made by
others.*]

[*There is a moment of stillness on the empty stage, then we
see a boy wandering into the light from* U R. *This is* JIM, *a
good-looking boy of seventeen. He is wearing a suit. His
tie is loose and his hands are in his trouser pockets. He is
strolling about, whistling the same air that was being
whistled earlier by the man with the packages. He gives an
impression of cheerful indolence. When he sees the packages, he stops, looks at them curiously for a moment, stirs
one with his foot casually, and finally bends over and picks
up from one of the packages that has fallen open, a large
wind-up animal. He gives a few twists to the key and cheerfully sends it on its way. As he watches the mechanical toy
in amused fashion, we suddenly hear the sound of a police
siren, close, loud, and getting closer. The lights go out.*]

[*When the lights come up, they reveal the area* L, *where the furniture consists of a bench, slightly upstage in the* L *area, facing the audience. A small table or desk is to the left, facing right. A police* OFFICER *in shirt sleeves is sitting behind the desk.* JIM *is standing up in front of the desk. Seated on the bench are* JUDY, PLATO, *and* MRS. DAVIS. JUDY *is a sixteen-year-old girl, attractive, but with a bitter, sullen expression. She is all dressed up.* JOHN PLATO CRAWFORD, *about fifteen, is wearing slacks and a sport shirt. He is cold and shivers slightly.* MRS. DAVIS *is a colored woman.* RAY, *a sympathetic juvenile officer, is standing at the upstage side of the desk, speaking to the* OFFICER.]

RAY. What's this one here for?

OFFICER. Headquarters sent him down.

RAY. Mixed up in that beating on Twelfth Street?

OFFICER. Picked up on suspicion. They had him on the carpet for an hour down at headquarters. He's clear.

RAY. Why didn't they send him home?

OFFICER. He tried to run away from the arresting squad.

RAY. I see. Well, I'll talk to him when I get through with these other two. [*Addresses* JIM.] Would you mind waiting for me, son? I want to talk to you before I send you home.

OFFICER. You want to leave him around here—leave him over there. [*Gestures toward bench.* JIM *shrugs, turns away, and crosses over to bench, where he sits down.*]

RAY [*returning papers he holds to desk and picking up another set, crossing to* JUDY]. Will you come with me, please?

JUDY [*looking up*]. Me?

RAY. Yes. [*Without a word,* JUDY *stands, preparing to follow him. They disappear into darkness, toward* C. *The* C *area spot comes on. The* L *area may be dimmed slightly and the characters remain inactive. We see two chairs in the* C *area.* RAY *indicates that one is for* JUDY *and moves it slightly. She sits down, in chair to the left, and he takes other chair.*] You're Judy, aren't you?

JUDY [*talking almost to herself*]. He hates me.

RAY. What?

JUDY [*to* RAY *this time*]. He hates me. [*Turns away from him.*]

RAY. What makes you think he hates you, Judy?

JUDY. I don't think. I know. He looks at me like I was the ugliest thing in the world. He doesn't like my friends—he doesn't like anything about me. He calls me, he calls . . . [*Starts to cry, burying her head in her hands on back of chair.*]

RAY [*after brief pause*]. He makes you feel pretty unhappy?

JUDY [*crying*]. He calls me a dirty tramp—my own father!

RAY. Do you think your father means that?

JUDY [*turning to face him*]. Yes! . . . I don't know! I mean, maybe he doesn't mean it but he acts like he does. We're all together and we're going to celebrate Easter and catch a double bill. Big deal. So I put on my new dress and I came out and he——

RAY. That one?

JUDY. Yes. He started yelling for a handkerchief—screaming. He grabbed my face, and he rubbed all my lipstick off. He rubbed till I thought I wouldn't have any lips left. And all the time yelling at me—that thing—the thing I told you he called me. Then I ran out of the house.

RAY. Is that why you were wandering around at one o'clock in the morning?

JUDY. I was just taking a walk. I called the kids but everybody was out, and I couldn't find them. I hate my life! I just hate it!

RAY. You weren't looking for company, were you?

JUDY. No.

RAY. Did you stop to talk to anyone, Judy? [JUDY *is silent.*] Do you enjoy that?

JUDY. No. I don't even know why I do it.

RAY. Do you think you can get back at your dad that way? [*As* JUDY *hesitates.*] I mean, sometimes if we can't get as close to somebody as we'd like, we have to try making them jealous—so they'll have to pay attention. Did you ever think of that?

JUDY [*bitterly*]. I'll never get close to *anybody*.

RAY. Some kids stomped a man on Twelfth Street, Judy.

JUDY. You know where they picked me up! *Twelfth* Street! I wasn't even *near* there!

RAY. Would you like to go home if we can arrange it? [JUDY *doesn't answer.*] Your parents haven't been notified. You wouldn't give the matron your phone number. Will you tell me, Judy? We'll see if your dad will come and get you. [JUDY *looks up hopefully.*] Unless you don't want to go home. . . . [*Pauses a moment, but* JUDY *doesn't answer.*] Would you rather stay here?

JUDY [*quietly*]. Lexington 0-5549.

RAY [*rising*]. You go back in the other room and wait on the bench. I'll phone. [JUDY *rises abruptly and walks back to* L *area, where she resumes her seat on bench. At same time, lights come up in this area to former brightness.* RAY *leaves* C *area to make his phone call. He goes out* U C *as lights* C *dim. A siren is heard in distance.* JIM, *sitting on bench as* JUDY *enters, opens his mouth and starts to imitate it, a long, forlorn wail.* PLATO *smiles faintly at* JIM. MRS. DAVIS *just looks.* JUDY *ignores him.*]

OFFICER [*looking up*]. Hey! [JIM *continues.* OFFICER *shouts.*] *Hey!* That's enough static out of you.

JIM [*brashly*]. Want me to imitate a stupid cop?

OFFICER. Cut it out now. I'm warning you.

JIM [*pretending meekness*]. Yes, ma'am. [PLATO *pulls up his shirt collar and puts his arms across his chest as if cold.*]

MRS. DAVIS. You shiverin', John? You cold? [PLATO *shakes his head.* JIM *notices him.*]

JIM. Want my coat? [PLATO *looks up at* JIM. JIM *continues.*] You want my coat? It's warm. [PLATO *wants it but shakes his head "no."*]

[RAY *enters from* U C *and comes into* L *area.*]

RAY [*to* JUDY]. Your mother will be down in a few minutes, Judy.

JUDY. What?

RAY. Your mother will be down in a few minutes.

JUDY [*startled and not understanding*]. My *mother?*

RAY [*to* OFFICER, *moving upstage of desk*]. She's being called for. [JUDY *rises.* JIM *whistles at her softly but audibly.*]

JUDY. You said you'd call my father.

RAY. Your father wasn't home. He was out looking for you.

JUDY. I'll hear about that!

RAY. Isn't it what you wanted, Judy?

JUDY [*with sudden intensity*]. I don't *know.* I don't *know* what I want. [*Stops, glances around in an embarrassed fashion, and then continues.*] Is there somewhere I can wait —alone?

RAY. Certainly. Wait in the office—back there. [*Gestures off* D L. JUDY *starts* D L *quickly.*] Good-by, Judy. Take it easy. [JUDY *goes out* D L. RAY *turns and speaks to* PLATO.] John Crawford.

MRS. DAVIS. Yes, sir.

RAY. Come with me, John. [PLATO *rises and follows* RAY *into* C *area, as lights come up there, and dim in* L *area.* MRS. DAVIS *follows.* JIM *is alone on bench. He closes his eyes, throws his head back, and gives another siren wail.* OFFICER *ignores it.* RAY *and* PLATO, *with* MRS. DAVIS *following, have entered* C *area.* PLATO *sits in chair, facing downstage.* MRS. DAVIS *seats herself in chair that was occupied by Judy.* RAY *stands a little to the right and slightly downstage of* PLATO. *After they have seated themselves,* RAY *speaks.*] Do you know why you shot those puppies, John? [*Silence.*] Is that what they call you or do you have a nickname?

PLATO [*murmuring*]. Plato.

MRS. DAVIS [*giving* PLATO'S *arm a little tug*]. Talk to the man nice now, you hear? He's goin' to help you.

PLATO. Nobody can help me.

RAY. Can you tell me why you killed the puppies, Plato?

PLATO. No, sir. I just went next door to look at them like I always do. They were nursing on their mother, and I did it. I guess I'm just no good.

RAY. What do you think's going to happen, you do things like that?

PLATO. I don't know. End up in the electric chair?

RAY. Where did you get the gun?

PLATO. In my mother's drawer.

MRS. DAVIS. She keeps it to protect herself, sir. She scared without a man in the house.

RAY. Where's your mother tonight, Plato?

PLATO. Away.

MRS. DAVIS [*shaking her head*]. Seems like she's always goin'. She got a sister in Chicago and she went for the holiday. She say her sister's all the family she has.

RAY. Where's your father? [PLATO *is silent, his head lowered.*]

MRS. DAVIS. They not together, sir. We don't see him a long time now.

RAY. Do you hear from him, son? [*Continues to* MRS. DAVIS *as* PLATO *doesn't respond.*] You know if the boy ever talked to a psychiatrist?

PLATO [*smiling a bit, looking up*]. Head-shrinker?

MRS. DAVIS [*laughing*]. Oh, Mrs. Crawford don't believe in them!

RAY. Well, maybe she better start.

PLATO. Don't want anything to do with one of them nut doctors.

RAY. Why not?

PLATO. I don't believe in them.

RAY [*to* MRS. DAVIS]. I want to talk to this boy's mother when she returns.

MRS. DAVIS. She'll be back Tuesday, for sure.

RAY. The owner of the dog isn't going to press charges. You can take Plato home, providing his mother comes in to see me when she gets back.

MRS. DAVIS [*rising*]. I'll certainly do that. You can depend on me, sir. [*To* PLATO.] You come along with me now, but thank this gentleman, you hear?

PLATO [*rising*]. Thank you very much, sir. I'm sorry.

RAY. That's all right, son. We all have crazy impulses. What you've got to remember is the difference between people who are in trouble and people who are getting along all right is just that the people who are getting along all right don't give in. [*Escorts* PLATO *and* MRS. DAVIS *to area* L, *as lights brighten here and dim in* C *area. This occurs during his speech. Now he addresses seated* OFFICER.] This boy is free to go. [*Marks paper he has been carrying and returns it to desk.*]

[*As* PLATO *and* MRS. DAVIS *go out* D L, JIM'S *parents, Mr. and Mrs. Stark* (MOTHER *and* FATHER) *and Mr. Stark's mother* (GRANDMA), *enter* D L. JIM, *on the bench, ignores them, humming "The Ride of the Valkyries" to himself.*]

MOTHER [*offstage* D L]. Jim! [JIM *looks up suddenly, scared. Then he smiles mysteriously and jumps to his feet.* MOTHER, FATHER, *and* GRANDMA *are framed in entrance, frozen. They are all well dressed in party clothes.* MOTHER *is a very chic but rather hard-faced woman.* FATHER *is a man always unsure of himself.* GRANDMA *is the smallest, also very chic and very bright-eyed.* RAY *has paused by upstage side of desk again.*]

JIM [*facing them*]. Happy Easter.

MOTHER [*as she,* FATHER, *and* GRANDMA *move toward him*]. Where were you tonight? They called us at the club, and I got the fright of my life! [*Silence.*]

FATHER. Where were you tonight, Jimbo? [JIM *says nothing.* FATHER *laughs uncomfortably.*]

JIM [*nodding toward* RAY]. Ask him.

FATHER [*to* RAY]. Was he drinking? I don't see what's so bad about taking a little drink.

RAY. You don't?

FATHER. No. I definitely don't. I did the sa——

RAY. He's a minor, Mr. Stark, and he hasn't been drinking. He was picked up on suspicion at the scene of a stomping.

FATHER. A what?

RAY. A gang of teen-agers beat up a man.

FATHER. Why?

RAY. For the fun of it.

FATHER. Was Jim involved?

RAY. He was at the scene just after it happened. We had to be sure. It's serious.

MOTHER. What do you mean, "serious"?

RAY. The man's in the hospital. He's in bad condition.

FATHER. But Jim hasn't done anything. You said so.

RAY. That's right.

FATHER. After all, a little drink isn't much. I cut pretty loose in my day, too.

MOTHER [*needling him*]. Really, Frank? When was that?

FATHER [*blowing up*]. Listen, *can't you wait till we get home?*

RAY [*holding up his hand*]. Whoa! Whoa! I know you're a little upset, but——

FATHER. Sorry.

RAY. What about you, Jim? Got anything to say for yourself? [JIM *stops humming and shrugs.*] Not interested, huh? [JIM *shakes his head.*]

MOTHER. Can't you answer? What's the matter with you?

FATHER. He's in one of his moods.

MOTHER [*to* FATHER]. I was talking to *Jim*.

FATHER [*crossing to* RAY]. Let me explain. We just moved here, y'understand? The kid has no friends yet and——

JIM. Tell him why we moved here.

FATHER. Hold it, Jim.

JIM. You can't protect me.

FATHER [*to* JIM]. You mind if I *try?* You have to slam the door in my face? [*To* RAY.] I try to get to him. What happens? [*To* JIM.] Don't I give you everything you want? A bicycle—you get a bicycle. A car——

JIM. You buy me many things. [*A little mock bow.*] Thank you.

FATHER. Not just buy! You hear all this talk about not loving your kids enough. We give you love and affection, don't we? [*Silence.* JIM *is fighting his emotion.*] Then what is it? I can't even touch you any more but you pull away. I want to understand you. You must have reasons. [JIM *stares straight ahead, trying not to listen.*] Was it because we went to that party? [*Silence.*] You know what kind of drunken brawls those parties turn into. It's no place for kids.

MOTHER. A minute ago you said you didn't care if *he* drinks.

GRANDMA. He said a *little* drink.

JIM [*exploding*]. Let me alone! [*Moves down right in* L *area.*]

MOTHER. What?

JIM. Stop tearing me apart! You say one thing, and he says another, and then everybody changes back——

MOTHER. That's a fine way to talk!

GRANDMA [*smiling*]. Well, you know whom he takes after!

RAY [*moving to* JIM]. Come into the next room. [*Indicates area* C *where he has been talking to Judy and Plato. Then he turns to others.*] Excuse us a minute?

FATHER [*very overwrought*]. Sure. Sure. [RAY *and* JIM *go into the* C *area, as lights come up.* FATHER, MOTHER, *and* GRANDMA, *after looking around uncertainly, sit down on bench. Lights now dim slightly in this area.*]

JIM [*nodding backward toward other room*]. Someone should put poison in her epsom salts.

RAY. Grandma? [*No answer.* JIM *turns away from* RAY.]

JIM. Get lost.

RAY. Hang loose, boy. I'm warning you.

JIM. Wash up and go home.

RAY. Big tough character. You don't kid me, pal. How come you're not wearing your boots? [*Suddenly* JIM *flings himself at* RAY, *who deftly flips him past and drops him on floor.* RAY *continues.*] Too bad you didn't connect. You could have gone to Juvenile Hall. That's what you want, isn't it?

JIM [*rising*]. No.

RAY. Sure, it is. You want to bug us till we have to lock you up. Why?

JIM. Leave me alone.

RAY. No.

JIM. I don't know why——[*Sits in right chair.*]

RAY [*standing behind other chair*]. Go on—don't give me that. Someone giving you hard looks?

JIM. I just get so——[*Fights tears.*] Boy, sometimes the temperature goes way up.

RAY [*suddenly gentle*]. Okay. Okay. Let it out. [JIM *starts crying, his face in his hands. There is a pause before* RAY *continues.*] You feel like you want to blow your wheels right now?

JIM. All the time! I don't know what gets into me, but I keep looking for trouble and I always——You better lock me up. I'm going to smash somebody—I know it.

RAY. Hit something. [JIM *smashes one fist against open palm of other hand.* RAY *watches, then sits in other chair.*] That why you moved from the last town? 'Cause you were in trouble? [*A pause.*] You can talk about it if you want to— I know about it anyway. Routine check.

JIM. And they think they are protecting me by moving.

RAY. Were you trying to stay out of trouble when you ran from the squad car?

JIM. It seemed like a good idea at the time.

RAY. According to their report, you weren't very cooperative at headquarters.

JIM. I told them everything I knew.

RAY. They weren't satisfied.

JIM. No. I didn't do anything, and already I'm in trouble. [*Glances* L.] Look at them out there.

RAY. You were getting a good start in the wrong direction before you moved to this city. Why did you do it?

JIM. Beat that fellow up? [RAY *just nods.* JIM *continues.*] He called me chicken.

RAY. And your folks didn't understand?

JIM. They never do.

RAY. So then you moved?

JIM. They think I'll make friends if we move. Just *move* and everything'll be roses and sunshine.

RAY. But you don't think that's a solution. [JIM *is silent; he picks at his nails.* RAY *continues.*] Things pretty tough for you at home?

JIM. She eats him alive and he takes it. [*Slaps side of his head.*] What a zoo!

RAY. What?

JIM. A zoo. He always wants to be my pal, you know. [*Gets up.*] But how can I give him anything when he's——I mean, I love him and I don't want to hurt him, but I don't know what to do any more except maybe die.

RAY. Pretty mixed up?

JIM. If he could——

RAY. "If he could" what? You mean your father?

JIM. I mean, if he had the guts to knock Mom cold once, I bet she'd be happy and I bet she'd stop picking. They make mush out of him. Just mush. One thing I know is, I never want to be like him.

RAY [*interrupting*]. Chicken?

JIM. I bet you see right through me, don't you? [RAY *shrugs.* JIM *sits again.*] How can anyone grow up in this circus?

RAY. You got me, Jim—but they do.

JIM [*shaking his head*]. Boy—if I had one day when I didn't have to be all confused and ashamed of everything—or if I just belonged some place.

RAY. Here. Look, will you do something for me? If the pot starts boiling again, come and see me before you get yourself in a jam? Come in and shoot the breeze. It's easier sometimes than talking to your folks.

JIM. Okay.

RAY. Any time—day or night. You calmed down enough to go back now?

JIM [*smiling*]. You serious? [RAY *crosses toward area* L *as lights come up.* JIM *follows. As he comes into lighted area* L, MOTHER *rises.* JIM *hesitates and then forces himself to cross over and kiss her. Area* C *dims and goes out completely.*]

JIM. I'm sorry.

MOTHER. All right, darling. [*Takes his arm. She and* JIM *start* D L, *followed by* GRANDMA *and* FATHER.]

GRANDMA [*pausing to speak to* RAY]. This was all very unfortunate, but he made a mistake and he's sorry—so we're not going to have any more trouble. He's always been a lovely boy.

JIM. Lovely! Grandma, if you tell another lie, you're going to turn to stone.

RAY. Luck, Jim. Don't forget.

FATHER [*offering* RAY *three cigars*]. Have some cigars.

RAY. No, thanks, I don't smoke.

FATHER [*forcing them on him*]. Go on—give 'em to your friends.

RAY. No—thanks very much, Mr. Stark.

MOTHER [*sharply*]. Frank—he doesn't want any. [JIM *grins at* RAY, *who nods.* MOTHER, JIM, FATHER, *and* GRANDMA *go out* D L, RAY *looking after them.* RAY *lights a cigarette and shakes his head as he stands in front of desk.*]

OFFICER. What a way to raise a kid.

RAY. How do you mean that?

OFFICER. Give him everything he wants and nothing he needs.

RAY. What does he need?

OFFICER. It's too late now, but instead of throwing bikes and cars at him, a strap on the behind when he got uppity would've saved them a lot of grief.

RAY. You figure he'll be back?

OFFICER. Hell, yes! He's got modern parents. They let him develop his personality. No inhibitions—no repressions!

RAY. A nice theory.

OFFICER. A theory for people who aren't tough enough to supply the back of the hand when it's needed. You juvenile counselors are wasting your time.

RAY. Maybe it's better to do a poor job of being too kind than a poor job of being too tough.

OFFICER. Listen, everybody needs discipline. I'm a "cop." It's what I get paid for, and, brother, cops will always have work.

RAY [*shrugging*]. I'm a cup of water—I can't put out any forest fire, but once in a while even a cup of water will do an important job—if it's early enough—in the right spot. [*Lights go out L area. Stage is in darkness.*]

[*A moment later the lights come up on R area, revealing a round (or oval) breakfast table set for four. MOTHER is seated upstage of the table, facing the audience, drinking a cup of coffee while she opens and reads the mail. As the light comes up, FATHER enters D R with two plates in his hand. He passes one directly across the table to the place on the left.*]

FATHER [*calling as he enters*]. Jim, your eggs are on the table. [*Sits down, at right of table.*] Anything in the mail?

MOTHER. No, dear. Mainly bills.

FATHER. I hope it goes well.

MOTHER. What?

FATHER. His first day at this new school.

MOTHER. Oh, that—of course it will.

[*JIM enters U R C, dressed in tie, jacket, and slacks.*]

MOTHER [*continuing, to* JIM]. Sit down and eat. You'll be late.

JIM [*pausing left of table*]. It'd stick in my throat, Mom. I'm nervous or something——

[GRANDMA *enters* D R *with a plate of toast.*]

GRANDMA. Have some more toast. [*Places it in front of* FATHER, *then pauses right of him.*]

FATHER [*to* GRANDMA]. Ma, you ought to sit down and eat something, yourself.

MOTHER. Don't keep after your mother that way. She *enjoys* getting breakfast for us.

GRANDMA [*to* MOTHER]. You could do with a little yourself. Orange juice and coffee!

MOTHER [*continuing, to* JIM, *who is still standing*]. At least have some milk.

JIM [*reaching over and picking up his glass of milk*]. I guess I'd better. It may settle my stomach.

GRANDMA. It's a wonder we don't all have lung cancer or some other terrible disease after living in all those smoky cities.

JIM [*cheerfully*]. They weren't so bad, Grandma.

GRANDMA [*sitting at downstage side of table*]. There aren't so many factories here.

FATHER. Mother——

JIM [*still standing*]. I'll need some dough.

FATHER. Of course, Jim. There is always something different you have to buy. [*Takes out his wallet and passes over a couple of dollar bills.*] This ought to cover it with a little left over for gas.

JIM. Thanks, Dad. [*Pockets bills.*]

FATHER. While you're walking off nervous energy, step outside and see if the paper was delivered.

JIM [*gulping his milk first, then putting glass down on table*]. Right away. [*Crosses toward* C *as light comes up in the* C *area, dimming in* R *area.*]

[In the c *area we find* JUDY, *dressed for school, calling back over her shoulder as she comes into the lighted area from* U L. *She carries some schoolbooks.]*

JUDY. All right, Belle. Go to school alone!

JIM *[to* JUDY*]*. Hey! *[*JUDY *ignores him, moving slightly past him.* JIM *continues.]* Hey, didn't I see you before some place? *[*JUDY *turns, looks at him with cold indifference, and turns her head away.]*

BELLE *[offstage* U L*]*. I'm coming, Judy. Just a minute.

JIM. I know I saw you before.

JUDY *[looking at him over her shoulder]*. Bully for you!

JIM. You don't have to be unfriendly.

JUDY. Now that's true!

JIM *[smiling]*. See?

JUDY. "Life is crushing in on me."

JIM *[smiling]*. "Life can be beautiful." Hey, I know where it was.

JUDY. Where what was?

JIM. Where I saw you. *[No answer.]* Everything going okay now? *[No answer.]* You live around here?

JUDY *[relieved]*. Who lives?

JIM. See, I'm new.

JUDY. Won't Mother be proud.

JIM. You're really flipped, aren't you? *[*JUDY *looks up, a little surprised.* JIM *continues.]* Where's Dawson High School?

JUDY. You going there?

JIM. Yeah—why?

JUDY *[looking him up and down]*. Dig the square wardrobe!

JIM *[defensively]*. Yeah. So where's the high school?

JUDY *[softer]*. University and 10th. Want to carry my books?

JIM. I was just getting my car. I could take you.

JUDY. The kids take me.

JIM. What kind of place is it?

JUDY *[shrugging]*. Crummy.

JIM. You don't like it?

JUDY. This afternoon there's a field trip.

JIM. Where?

JUDY. The planetarium.

JIM. What's it like?

JUDY. I never went.

JIM. For everybody?

JUDY. Just seniors.

JIM. Where is this?

JUDY. Out by the park.

JIM. Can you drive or do you go by bus?

JUDY. Either.

JIM. I could drive you. [*There is a long, long auto horn sound in distance.*]

JUDY. No. You'd better not. It's all arranged.

JIM. Oh. [*Horn now sounds nearby, impatiently, offstage* D L.]

JUDY [*her attitude changing, hard again*]. I'll bet you're a real yo-yo.

JIM. What?

JUDY [*yelling over sound of horn, starting* D L]. Good-by! See you!

JIM [*yelling back*]. I'm not so bad. [JUDY *goes out* D L. JIM *looks after her a moment, then turns and crosses* U R C *as* C *area light goes out. He picks up a paper in dark area* U R C *and re-enters lighted area at* R *in which the lights have been dim through previous scene. He speaks cheerfully.*] Here's the paper, Dad. [*Comes left of table and hands it across table to* FATHER; *continues to* MOTHER.] You make any sandwiches? [MOTHER *rises and goes out* D R.]

FATHER. My first day of school, Mother'd make me eat, and by golly, I could never even swallow till recess.

[MOTHER *re-enters* D R *with a brown paper bag of lunch.*]

MOTHER [*moving upstage of table again*]. There's nothing to be nervous about. [*Hands bag to him.*] Here's peanut butter and meat loaf. [JIM *makes a mouth-stuck-together-with-pea-nut-butter motion with his mouth.*]

GRANDMA. What did I tell you? Peanut butter!

MOTHER. Well, there's a thermos of orange juice and some applesauce cake in the wax paper to wash it down.

GRANDMA. I baked that!

JIM [*kissing* MOTHER *on cheek*]. 'By, Mom.

MOTHER. Good-by, dear.

FATHER [*rising*]. So long, young fella. Knock 'em dead, like your old man used to!

JIM. Sure. [*Moves toward* C, *stops, and turns.*] You know something? I have a feeling we're going to stay here.

FATHER. And listen—watch out about the pals you choose. Know what I mean? Don't let them choose you. [*But* JIM *is on his way out* D L. MOTHER *starts to sit as lights go out.*]

[*The lights come up in the* C *area again, disclosing several rows of folding chairs, arranged in a semi-circle facing the audience. At* D L C *is a small podium. It is the intermission of the planetarium lecture, and the students are returning to their seats from the general direction of offstage* L, *talking and acting like high school students.* MISS HANNINGTON, *the teacher, is standing* D L C, *near the podium.*]

MISS HANNINGTON. Please! The intermission is over. I want you all to return to your seats. [*Speaks to one of the girls, who has paused to ask a question.*] No, Helen, sit wherever you please. You don't have to sit in the same position. [*Speaks louder.*] Quiet, everybody. Quiet, please! I'll be back in a moment with the lecturer and I want you all in your seats, ready. [*Goes out* L.]

[JUDY *enters the lighted area from* L. JIM, *who has been seated in one of the chairs, gets up and meets her* D C.]

JIM. Hi!

JUDY. You found it.

JIM. Where's your friend?

JUDY. Somebody wanted to ask him some questions.

JIM. I could drive you home.

JUDY. I said I'd wait.

JIM. He might not show up.

JUDY. So I'm late for dinner.

JIM. Maybe I should wait with you in case he doesn't come. This isn't an easy place to walk home from.

JUDY. Now that's a thought. What do you do when he does show up?

JIM. You don't have to wait. If he doesn't show, he doesn't show.

JUDY [*thoughtfully*]. You don't worry much.

JIM. I saved a seat for you. [*Takes a step toward down right edge of semi-circle of chairs and indicates two vacant chairs on end of first row.*]

JUDY. Be with you in a minute. I'll get my books. [*Crosses and goes out L again.*]

[*While JIM is waiting, PLATO has entered L and crosses over to him.*]

PLATO [*speaking uncertainly*]. Hi.

JIM [*glancing at him, friendly but indifferent*]. Hi, there.

PLATO. You remember me?

JIM [*looking at him for a second, puzzled but unperturbed*]. No, I don't think so.

PLATO [*suddenly withdrawn*]. I'm sorry. I guess I made a mistake. [*Heads for chairs and takes a seat on extreme right end of semi-circle in second row.*]

[*JUDY re-enters L with her books and rejoins JIM, who is watching PLATO. They cross over to the seats at the extreme end of the front row and sit down. BUZZ enters L just as they sit down together. He stands at the far left side of the lighted area, downstage, away from JUDY and JIM. He looks around and sees them after they have been seated next to each other. We recognize BUZZ by his clothes as the leader of the stomp gang from the first scene.*]

BUZZ [*loudly*]. Stella-a-a-a!

JUDY [*jumping up quickly, crossing to him*]. Steady, Marlon!

BUZZ [*making motion with his fingers*]. Wanna make the colored lights go around and around? [JUDY *and* BUZZ *kiss firmly but quickly and without interest.* BUZZ *looks over at* JIM, *then at* JUDY.] What's *that?*

JUDY. A new disease.

BUZZ [*a little suspicious*]. Friend of yours?

JUDY [*changing subject*]. Did they ask you much?

BUZZ. Plenty.

JUDY. I'm glad they let you out.

BUZZ. Nobody chickened.

JUDY. I heard about it. You're lucky he lived.

BUZZ. They always live. [*There is faint sound of music in background and lights dim slightly.* BUZZ *takes* JUDY *by the arm and leads her to two vacant chairs in center of first row.*]

[MISS HANNINGTON *re-enters* L *at this point.*]

MISS HANNINGTON [*moving toward* C]. Seats, please. In your *seats*, please! [*Remaining students sit.*] Before we start, I have two announcements. All students who came by bus must return to the bus immediately after the lecture. The bus will return you to the school. It isn't necessary to report back to your home room. [*Lights dim further.* MISS HANNINGTON *moves to a seat in back row and sits.*]

[*The lecturer (woman) enters* L *and steps to podium.*]

LECTURER [*as students subside*]. As we look once more and for the last time at the replica of the stars in their courses reflected on the dome of this planetarium in their everchanging but orderly pattern, we note that one of these stars is much larger than the rest and increases in size as we watch. [*Music of spheres is heard—a high threatening tremolo. Students are looking up, as though at dome of planetarium.* LECTURER'S *voice continues.*] As this star approaches us, the weather will change. The great polar fields of the north and south will rot and divide, and the seas will turn warmer.

[*Students sit, for the most part, entranced by* LECTURER *and faint background music.*] The familiar constellations that illuminate our night will seem as they have always seemed, eternal, unchanged, and little moved by the shortness of time between our planet's birth and its demise. Orion, the Hunter.
[LECTURER *makes frequent pauses during following.*]

JIM. Boy!

PLATO [*who is seated behind* JIM, *leaning forward*]. What?

JIM [*half turning, noticing who it is*]. I remember you. [*Continuing in a friendly fashion.*] Once you've been up here, you know you've been some place.

LECTURER. Gemini, the Twins. [*During this,* JUDY *has been watching program in interest and fascination.* BUZZ, *not at all interested, has an arm around* JUDY *and is nuzzling her ear.*]

BUZZ [*to* JUDY]. Hey. [*Pokes her. She looks at him. He curves his wrist toward her, opening and closing his first two fingers like the pincers of a crab.* JUDY *laughs, as do several of the students in their vicinity, particularly* CRUNCH *and* GOON. JIM *looks over at them and smiles.*]

LECTURER. Taurus, the Bull.

JIM [*contributing to fun*]. Moo! [*There is a silence finally broken by* CRUNCH.]

CRUNCH [*flatly*]. Yeah, moo.

BUZZ [*taking it up*]. Moo. That's real cute. Moo.

GOON. Hey, he's real rough!

CRUNCH. I'll bet he fights with cows.

BUZZ. Moo. [JUDY *smiles appreciatively at* JIM, *concealing her smile from* BUZZ.]

LECTURER [*continuing*]. Sagittarius and Aries—all as they have ever been.

PLATO [*leaning forward, touching* JIM *on shoulder, speaking softly*]. You shouldn't monkey with him.

JIM. Why?

PLATO. He's a wheel. So's she. It's hard to make friends with them.

JIM [*unhappy at having revealed himself, turning away from* PLATO]. I don't want to make friends.

LECTURER. And while the flash of our beginning has not yet traveled the light years into distance—has not yet been seen by planets deep within the other galaxies—we will disappear into the blackness of the space from which we came. [*Music is loud.*] Destroyed as we began, in a burst of gas and fire. [*Music reaches explosion.* LECTURER *continues.*] The heavens are still and cold once more. In all the complexity of our universe and the galaxies beyond, the Earth will not be missed. [*As he comes to an end, lights start to get bright, and we hear the beginning, softly, of "Morning Song" by Grieg.*] Through the infinite reaches of space, the problems of Man seem trivial and naive indeed. And Man, existing alone, seems to be an episode of little consequence. . . . That's all. Thank you very much. [*Music continues a little louder for a moment to a scattering of applause from students, and then fades away.* JIM *rises, turns, and ruffles* PLATO'S *hair.*]

JIM. Hey! It's over! The world's ended!

PLATO. What does he know about Man alone? [*While above speeches are going on,* BUZZ *rises and starts to cross toward* JIM, *while* JIM *is talking to* PLATO. BUZZ *stops, looks around, goes back, and talks to* CRUNCH, GOON, *and* MOOSE. JUDY, HELEN, *and* MILLIE *listen. Then the boys move out* L *in a unit.* JUDY *goes out* L *with them.* HELEN *and* MILLIE *linger behind. While they do this, other students, milling and scattering, move out* L, *as individuals or in groups of two or more, and keeping a careful distance.*]

MISS HANNINGTON [*moving down to* LECTURER]. We'll be out of here in a minute. Maybe it would help if you turned the lights up.

LECTURER. Certainly. [*Clicks switch in podium and lights brighten so that almost the whole stage is lighted.*]

MISS HANNINGTON. Thank you. I'd better go and try to get them into the bus now. [*Hurries out* L. JIM *and* PLATO *follow out* L, *then the* LECTURER *leaves. Only* HELEN *and* MILLIE *are left behind.*]

HELEN. Judy started something.

MILLIE. She dropped the ball. Let's go see if it bounces.

HELEN. Buzz better be careful.

MILLIE. Come on. I want to see what happens.

HELEN. Do you think Judy's interested?

MILLIE. That's nothing. Buzz is just looking for an excuse. Helen, if we stay here too long, we'll have to ride home in the bus with the creeps. [*Both shudder at thought, and turn to go.*]

[*At this point,* JIM *enters from* L, *stops a moment, is noticed by* MILLIE *and* HELEN *as he crosses and sits down in a chair at far right of the second row of chairs. He leans back in the chair, casually placing his feet on the chair in front of him as if to wait patiently. The girls look at him, and* HELEN *clucks softly like a chicken as she and* MILLIE *go out* L. JIM *listens, abruptly pulls his feet off the chair so that his chair bangs forward. He is all attention as they go out* L. *After they disappear, he resumes his previous position.* PLATO *comes running in from* L *and speaks almost hysterically as if he had been running from a fire.*]

PLATO [*moving toward* JIM]. What's your name?

JIM. Jim. What's yours?

PLATO [*a little quieter*]. Plato. It's a nickname. [*Sits down beside him.*] Listen, I told you not to fool with them. Now they're waiting for you.

JIM. I know. That's why I came back.

PLATO. You scared?

JIM. I just don't want trouble.

PLATO. He has a knife.

JIM. I saw it.

PLATO. What are you going to do?

JIM [*shrugging his shoulders*]. Wait here for a bit. It's sort of peaceful in here. [*Glances up.*] All that talk about the stars. It's hard to worry about things. [*There is a moment of silent communion between the two.*]

PLATO [*looking around during this moment of silence to lecturer's podium, as if remembering what she had said; then he turns back, speaking anxiously*]. Jim?

JIM. I'm here.

PLATO. Jim, do you think when the end of the world comes it will be at night?

JIM. No. In the morning. [PLATO *looks at him questioningly.* JIM *smiles, shrugs his shoulders, and adds:*] I just have a feeling.

PLATO. If you don't want trouble, I know a place we can go. There's a way out of here the personnel uses. We would keep the building between us and your car and get over to the bus line without being seen. The busses are going now.

JIM. You don't want me to leave my car?

PLATO. You'll have to. They slashed your tires. Come on, Jim. Let's get out of here. [*Rises.*] We'd better get going. [*Glances apprehensively* L.]

JIM [*quietly, still seated*]. It's late.

[*At this point,* BUZZ, *closely followed by the gang,* CRUNCH, GOON *and* MOOSE, *as well as* HELEN, MILLIE, *and* JUDY, *enter* L. *Their appearance is similar in manner to their appearance in the opening scene. They appear in a silent group and pause at* L. *As* BUZZ *and the others enter,* JIM *looks around* PLATO *to see them as they come in.* PLATO *notices this and turns to face them. He looks back at* JIM, *then over at the group, who stand ominously and silent.*]

PLATO [*almost stuttering with fear, to* JIM]. I-I-I got to go. [*Edges toward* U L.]

BUZZ [*to* PLATO]. What you looking for?

PLATO [*still frightened*]. Nothing. [*Edges down around* BUZZ *and bolts out* L.]

BUZZ [*to* JIM]. I've been waiting for you.

JIM [*still seated*]. I know.

BUZZ. By your car.

JIM. Shrewd.

BUZZ. You got four flat tires. I slashed 'em.

JIM [*wearily*]. You know somethin'?

BUZZ. What?

JIM [*reproachfully*]. You watch too much television.

BUZZ [*to group*]. Hey, he's real abstract and different.

JIM. I'm cute, too. [*Suddenly* GOON *starts clucking softly like a chicken. One by one, others pick it up. Group moves slightly toward* C. BUZZ *at last crows.* JIM *speaks.*] Meaning me?

BUZZ. What?

JIM. Chicken. [*Group laughs shortly.* JIM *takes off his glasses, smiles, shakes his head disapprovingly.*] You shouldn't call me that. [*Walks across to* BUZZ, *standing right next to him. As he does, group gathers around to watch developing action. As they do,* JUDY *becomes evident just upstage of* BUZZ. JIM, *a foot from* BUZZ, *stops and turns to* JUDY.] You always at ringside? You always travel in this rank company? [*Nods toward* BUZZ. BUZZ *clutches* JIM'S *hair, jerks his head forward, and slaps him in face with his open hand.* JIM *jerks free, ready to fight, takes a step toward* BUZZ, *who has retreated.* JIM *stops dead as* BUZZ *draws and opens a knife.*] I thought only punks fought with knives?

BUZZ. Who's fighting? This is the test, man. It's a crazy game.

HELEN. Les jeux de courage!

CRUNCH [*wetting his lips*]. Machismo. Machismo.

JIM. Machismo?

BUZZ. Somebody find him a knife. [*Group forms in a semi-circle* D C. *Somebody tosses an open knife so it sticks into floor of stage near* JIM. JIM *stoops and picks up his weapon, then faces* BUZZ.] You know the action? No cutting. Just sticking—jab real cool. [*They begin stalking each other.* BUZZ *slides his knife from hand to hand, trying to hypnotize*

JIM. *Suddenly he pokes out and pricks* JIM's *shirt. The group sighs "Olé!"* JIM *makes no effort at self-defense. Silence.* BUZZ *pricks* JIM *again. Group shouts "Olé!"* BUZZ *maneuvers.*] What you waiting on, Toreador? I thought you wanted some action! [JIM *cuts out half-heartedly.* BUZZ *sidesteps.*] Big brave bull. Hah! Toro! Hah! Hah!

GOON. Moo!

BUZZ. Come on! Fascinate us! Impress us! What's happening? Let's go!

JIM. I don't want trouble.

BUZZ [*suddenly furious*]. You crud chicken! You're wasting our time! [*Viciously, he slaps* JIM *across face.* JIM *lashes out and misses.* BUZZ *hops back.*] Yeah—that's pretty close. How about a little closer, Toreador? Cut off a button and you get to join the club!

[PLATO *appears* L, *swinging a length of tire chain.**]

PLATO [*coming to a stop at down left edge of group, addressing all of group as well as* JIM *and* BUZZ]. Break! [*Almost screams.*] Break, I tell you!

MILLIE. Buzzie, look out! He's got a chain! [JIM *and* BUZZ *continue to circle carefully.*]

BUZZ [*stepping back for a minute as* MILLIE *speaks, and looking at* PLATO, *calling out cheerfully*]. Hey! Chicken Little! [*At this* PLATO *raises chain, starts to swing it down, and rushes in.* BUZZ *expertly steps out of way, trips him, and delivers a vicious kick to the fallen* PLATO, *who covers his head and huddles on floor.* JIM, *who has stepped back to watch this, suddenly is transformed. The moment* BUZZ *looks up,* JIM *bores forward, expertly pricking* BUZZ *repeatedly on arms and occasionally the chest. Cries of "Olé!" greet him.* BUZZ *falls back in surprised caution. The only sound for a moment is the rapid breathing of the contestants.*]

---

*See Production Notes at back of playbook.

[MISS HANNINGTON *and the* LECTURER *appear* L. *They pause* D L, *conversing in pantomime.*]

CRUNCH [*who has been serving as a lookout, and glancing around occasionally, spots them, and calls*]. Honk! Let's split! [JIM *and* BUZZ *stop and look around edge of spectators.* PLATO *gets slowly to his feet.*]

BUZZ. Split for what? Couple old poop-heads? [*Folds up his knife and puts it away. So does* JIM.]

JIM. You satisfied or you want more?

BUZZ. How 'bout you? Say the word and you're cold, Jack—you're dead.

JUDY. Buzzie—we better get out of here.

BUZZ. What's eating you, Judy? You want him alive?

JIM. Where can we meet?

BUZZ. Know the Millertown bluff?

MILLIE. The bluff, Buzz! That's dangerous up there.

BUZZ. Draw him a picture, Chicken Little. Eight o'clock. Cookie, you and Moose get a couple cars. We're going to have us some real kicks. Little chickie-run. You been on chickie-runs before?

JIM. Sure—that's all I do. [MISS HANNINGTON *bursts in among group.* LECTURER *remains on fringe.*]

MISS HANNINGTON. All right. All of you—start moving!

JUDY. You mean li'l ol' us? What's the matter with the nice lady?

MISS HANNINGTON. Who said that? [*Looks at group. There is no response.*]

BUZZ [*while* MISS HANNINGTON'S *back is turned*]. Old hag, school's out. Go home and play with your dollies.

MISS HANNINGTON [*whirling toward him*]. Now that we've proved how brave we are by saying names behind my back, we will disperse, with no more nonsense. I may not be able to control you—[*Hesitates, then continues.*]—monsters outside of school, but while you're under my charge, you'll behave.

LECTURER. Don't lose control, Miss Hannington. I'm sure if we just explain——

MISS HANNINGTON. Explain to *these?* [*Shakes her head.*] They think they own the world.

CRUNCH. The world is round!

MILLIE. The world is flat!

MISS HANNINGTON. All right, let's go. [*Starts L.*]

HELEN [*following*]. All the world's a stage! [*There is wild laughter from group as they obediently follow after her, L, group commenting to show their independence as they go.*]

MILLIE. The world goes 'round the sun!

MOOSE. Good-by, proud world!

CRUNCH. I got the world on a string!

GOON. The world's my oyster!

HELEN. Hey! A fish-eater! Brain food. [*JIM stands still D C, as they go. He looks down at his shirt on which there are spots of blood. Only JIM, PLATO, and the LECTURER remain. PLATO moves to him, opens shirt, pulls out a handkerchief, spits on it, and starts to wipe blood away.*]

LECTURER [*smiling, moving toward D C*]. Sometimes the world is too much with us, isn't it, boy? What was the disturbance?

JIM. Nothing.

LECTURER. You're bleeding. Are you all right?

JIM [*brusquely*]. I scratched my mosquito bites. I'm fine. [*LECTURER hesitates. JIM repeats, in a tone of dismissal.*] I'm fine—*thanks!* [*LECTURER turns abruptly and goes out L.*]

PLATO. You going?

JIM. What's a chicken-run?

PLATO. You know that bluff he was talking about?

JIM. I think so.

PLATO. It's a big flat field with a cliff at the end.

JIM. Yeah?

PLATO. It's to see who's chicken. They steal a couple of cars. One guy in each car. They start off towards the cliff—going fast. Whoever jumps from his car first is chicken.

JIM [*calmly*]. Sounds dangerous.

PLATO. It is. [*Pauses.*] You going?

JIM [*shrugging*]. Who knows? [*Lights out.*]

CURTAIN

ACT TWO

AT RISE OF CURTAIN: *It is evening of the same day. The* L *area is lit. The scene is in Judy's home. In it is a dining-room table with four chairs around it.* JUDY *is finishing setting the table. She is preoccupied and pauses, moving* L. *She looks up and off in the direction of* L, *as if she were gazing out the dining-room window at the sky.* BELLE, *her fourteen-year-old younger sister, comes in* D L *with a pitcher of milk, puts it down on the table near the center, and looks over at* JUDY.]

BELLE [*pausing left of table*]. I brought in the milk for you.

JUDY. What? [*Turns from window.*]

BELLE. You're far out.

JUDY. Thanks for bringing the milk. I must have been thinking. Clear out of here when Dad comes. I've got to get out tonight.

BELLE. After Easter, I'm surprised you'd bring it up. Don't worry about me. I won't even be close. [*Ducks out* D L. JUDY *looks at table speculatively for a moment, turns, looks out window again.*]

[MR. BROWN, *Judy's father, enters from the darkness* U C, *comes above the table, and looks at* JUDY *for a moment.*]

MR. BROWN. What are you wishing for, Judy?

JUDY [*half-turning toward him, then speaking softly*]. I wasn't wishing—I was looking at the moon.

MR. BROWN [*crossing to behind her, looking out window over her shoulder, chanting*].

"Man in the Moon, how come you there
Up in the sky where you are shining,
Floating so high in the frosty air?
Oh, say—Man in the Moon!"

JUDY [*astonished, turning to face him*]. How did *you* know that?

MR. BROWN. We used to sing it in school. [*Smiles.*] Don't look at me with such horror. They had schools in those days.

JUDY. But the same song. I think it's fantastic!

MR. BROWN. We were romantic then, too.

JUDY. Are you and Mom home tonight?

MR. BROWN. No. Why?

JUDY. Nothing, only maybe it would be nicer to spend the evening at home together for a change.

MR. BROWN. Nicer than what?

JUDY. Nicer than nothing.

MR. BROWN. You wouldn't want to spend the evening with us old creeps. We're going out, and you've got to do your homework.

JUDY. I know, but——

MR. BROWN [*admonishing, but gently*]. You agreed to stay home on school nights.

JUDY. I know, Daddy, but——

MR. BROWN. Come on, we have to eat. [*Turns and crosses toward upstage chair at dining-room table.*]

JUDY [*quickly*]. You forgot something.

MR. BROWN [*turning toward her*]. What? [JUDY *doesn't answer but leans forward and kisses him quickly on the lips. He is shocked.*] What's the matter? [JUDY *steps back, a little frightened. He continues.*] You're too old for that kind of stuff, kiddo. I thought you stopped doing that sort of thing long ago.

JUDY [*hurt*]. I don't want to stop.

[MRS. BROWN *enters briskly from* D L.]

MRS. BROWN [*carrying two covered vegetable bowls, coming around to right of table, putting bowls on table*]. Don't want to stop what?

MR. BROWN. Nothing.

JUDY. I was talking to Dad.

MR. BROWN. I didn't kiss her, so it's a big thing.

MRS. BROWN [*calling to kitchen*]. Belle! Bring the soufflè! [*To* MR. BROWN.] Fish soufflè. [*To* JUDY.] You don't have to stand there, darling. Drink your tomato juice. [JUDY *slides into her chair at left side of table.* MR. BROWN *is now seated in chair at upstage side of table, and* MRS. BROWN *is at right side of table. The remaining chair, downstage, is for Belle.*]

JUDY. I guess I just don't understand anything.

MR. BROWN. I'm *tired*, Judy. I'd like to change the subject.

JUDY. Why?

MR. BROWN. I'd like to, that's all. Girls your age don't do that. You need an explanation?

JUDY [*very low*]. Girls don't love their fathers? Since when? Since I got to be sixteen? [*Half-rises to kiss him again.*]

MR. BROWN. Stop it now! Sit down! [*Slaps her.*]

[*There is a terrible silence, into which* BELLE *enters,* D L, *bringing with her the soufflè, which she sets in front of* MR. BROWN.]

MR. BROWN [*putting an arm around her*]. Hi, honey bun!

BELLE [*aware of strain, glancing about*]. Hi.

JUDY [*weeping, rising*]. May I please be excused? [*Starts* D L. MR. BROWN *rises and follows her.* JUDY *continues out* D L.]

MR. BROWN [*softly*]. Hey. Hey, glamorpuss! [*Pauses* D L *and calls after her.*] I'm sorry. [*Turns back to table and sits down.* MRS. BROWN *rises and comes to him.* MR. BROWN *continues.*] I don't know what to do. All of a sudden she's a problem. [MRS. BROWN *stands behind his chair. She tips his head back against her body and kneads his neck and shoulders.*]

MRS. BROWN. She'll outgrow it, dear. It's just the age.

BELLF [*in a sudden burst*]. The atomic age! [*Door slams off-stage* D L.]

MRS. BROWN [*kissing her husband's hair*]. It's the age when nothing fits. [*Lights go out on* L *area.*]

[*The lights come up again a moment later on the* R *area, another room in Jim's home. There is a couch, facing the audience. To the right of it is a small table with a lamp and an alarm clock. To the left of the couch, but slightly downstage of it, is an easy chair. As the lights come on, we see* JIM *sprawling on the couch, his feet toward the left end, awake, with his hands clasped behind his head. There is a moment of silence as he lies there thinking, and then the alarm clock goes off. He reaches behind him, turns it off, and sits up. As if in answer to the alarm, Jim's* FATHER *appears from* R, *wearing an apron and minus his suit coat.*]

FATHER. Did you set the alarm?

JIM. Yes.

FATHER [*pausing by table*]. I looked in earlier. It looked like you were taking a nap.

JIM. No, I wasn't asleep. Just thinking.

FATHER. Listen, I took a steak out of the freezer. I thought we could have a real old-fashioned stag party—just the two of us. What do you say?

JIM. I'm not hungry. [FATHER *turns away, disappointed.*] Hey —I want to ask you something.

FATHER [*happily, turning back*]. Shoot, Jimbo.

JIM. Suppose you knew that you had to do something very dangerous—where you have to prove something you need to know—a question of honor. Would you do it?

FATHER [*laughing*]. Is there some kind of trick answer?

JIM [*insistently*]. What would you do, Dad?

FATHER [*moving behind couch to left of it*]. "Honor"—that's quite a word. What do you mean by it?

JIM. Everyone knows that.

FATHER. I'm serious. Tell me—what do you mean?

JIM. Being a right guy. The kind of a fellow people can believe in. [*Pauses, then continues.*] Someone who, when he says something, means it.

FATHER. Is that all?

JIM. No. I left out one thing.

FATHER. What?

JIM. Guts.

FATHER. What kind of guts? Show-off or real?

JIM. Dad, you always try to give me reasons. There's a reason
for everything. If a guy's chicken, he can say he doesn't
want to show off or he doesn't want to upset his parents.
There's always a reason for anything anybody does. What I
need to know is, should I or shouldn't I? Yes or no—right
now.

FATHER [*evading*]. I wouldn't do anything hasty. Let's get a
little light on the subject. [*Crosses back in front of sofa to
table and turns on lamp. In the brightened light that results,
FATHER turns around and looks at JIM. JIM is in his bloody
shirt. FATHER moves in front of JIM, sits down in chair near
davenport in shock and surprise.*]

JIM [*as if to answer his inquiry*]. Blood.

FATHER. How'd that happen? What kind of trouble you in?

JIM. The kind we've been talking about. Can you answer me
now?

FATHER. Listen—nobody should make a snap decision. This
isn't something you just——We ought to consider all the
pros and cons.

JIM. We don't have time.

FATHER. We'll make time. Where's some paper? We'll make
a list and if we're still stuck, then we ought to get some ad-
vice. [*Goes over to table and, with his back to JIM, rummages through table drawer for a paper and pencil.*]

JIM. What *can* you do when you have to be a man?

FATHER. Well, now——

JIM. Just give me a direct answer! [*Pause.*] You going to stop
me from going, Dad?

FATHER [*looking up from his rummaging and pausing for a
moment*]. You know I never *stop* you from anything. Believe me, you're at a wonderful age. In ten years you'll look
back on this and wish you were a kid again.

JIM. Ten years? *Now*, Dad—I need an answer *now!*

FATHER. I just want to show you how foolish you are. [*At this point,* JIM *gets up, puts on his shoes from under couch, picks up his jacket from back of chair, and goes off into the darkness toward* U C. FATHER *continues talking as he turns back to table and rummages in drawer again.*] When you're older you'll laugh at yourself for thinking this is so important. Here's a paper. I've got a pencil right here. [*Straightens up and turns around, with piece of paper and pencil.*] We'll make a list. Jim! [*Looks around.*] Will you listen? You can't go out till we——[*Crosses to edge of lighted area, toward* C.] Jim! [*Calls again louder.*] Jim! [*Looks around for a moment, defeated, then hurls pad and pencil toward the couch.*]

[MOTHER *enters* R.]

MOTHER. What's the matter?

FATHER. I don't know. Jim's in trouble. [*Comes to chair.*]

MOTHER. What sort of trouble?

FATHER. I don't know. He went out. [*Slumps down in chair.*]

MOTHER [*standing over him*]. Didn't you ask?

FATHER [*flaring at her*]. Of course I asked. He didn't say.

MOTHER. Didn't you forbid his going out, then?

FATHER [*turning, with a moment of violence in his voice*]. No, I didn't forbid him to go out!

MOTHER. It would be so easy to keep him out of trouble if you just try.

FATHER. If it's so easy, I should think you'd take over when I've messed it up.

MOTHER. You know I wouldn't interfere once you've given a decision.

FATHER. I know nothing of the kind. It's easy to second-guess. The nice thing about that is, you're always right; but the thing that's even nicer is, you've got no responsibility for what happens—none at all—because you ducked the decision when it counted.

MOTHER [*with cold contempt*]. I don't really blame the boy. Sometimes I look at you, and it's a wonder he has any courage at all.

FATHER. When I taught him to drive, I said to myself over and over again, "It doesn't matter what he does now while I'm sitting here. What matters is what happens after I get out of the car." That takes another kind of guts and that's why I didn't stop him. Maybe I'm not much of a father, but I try, and that's more than you do. [*Stands up, pulls off apron, throws it in chair as lights go out.*]

[*Now the lights come up in the* C *area. Most of the gang is there. They include* GOON, CRUNCH, MOOSE, MILLIE, *and* HELEN. *They are roughly grouped around* BUZZ *and* JUDY, *who are eating hamburgers.* BUZZ *and some of the others may have changed from their previous outfits into blue jeans and sport shirts.* PLATO *wanders into the lighted area from* U L, *looking searchingly for* JIM.]

BUZZ [*spotting him and calling*]. Hey, Chicken Little! [PLATO *stops.*] Where's Toreador? He beg off?

PLATO. He's not scared of you. [*Pauses left in lighted area, away from crowd.*]

BUZZ [*laughing*]. Yeah? [*To* GOON.] Goon! You seen that adolescent type anywheres?

CRUNCH. He won't show.

GOON. Well, you going to wait all night? I'm getting nervous, man! We got to *do* something!

HELEN [*calling over to* BUZZ]. You figure he left town? [BUZZ *looks at her coldly for a moment, then shakes his head, and turns back to* JUDY. HELEN *and* MILLIE *separate from group and wander to extreme* D L C *edge of stage.*]

MILLIE [*looking over and down*]. It's a long way down.

HELEN. "The sea is smooth tonight. The moon lies fair upon the straits."

MILLIE. Don't be a jerk. That's just the ocean down there.

HELEN. Yeah, I know. Where do you start from?

MILLIE [*pointing* U L]. There. They get in their cars back there and head for the cliff.

HELEN [*turning downstage again and looking over footlights and down*]. It's a long way down. [*Walks back into crowd, followed by* MILLIE.]

CRUNCH [*looking toward* U R]. Hey, Buzz!

BUZZ. What?

CRUNCH. Over there. [BUZZ *faces around toward* U R.]

[JIM *can be seen entering* U R. *He has just stepped into the edge of the lighted area.* PLATO *runs over to* JIM.]

JIM [*to* PLATO]. How'd *you* get here?

PLATO. I hitched.

JIM. Boy, I bet you'd go to a hanging.

PLATO. My personality's showing again. Should I leave?

JIM. No. It's okay. [BUZZ *crosses to* JIM.]

BUZZ. Come on. Let's see what we're driving. [JIM *follows* BUZZ *to* D L *corner of stage.* BUZZ *turns around as* PLATO *starts to follow.*] Just him.

JIM [*to* PLATO]. Stay here. [JIM *and* BUZZ *move out* D L. PLATO *looks after them, hurt, then goes over to* JUDY, *who is still standing at* C.]

JUDY [*to* PLATO]. Is he your friend?

PLATO. Yes. My *best* friend.

JUDY. What's he like?

PLATO. Oh, I don't know. You have to get to know him. He doesn't say much, but when he does, you know he means it. He's sincere.

JUDY. Well, that's the main thing. Don't you think so?

PLATO. Maybe next summer he's going to take me hunting with him—and fishing. I want him to teach me how, and I bet he won't get mad if I goof. His name's Jim. It's really James, but he likes Jim more. [*Laughs.*] People he really likes—he lets call him "Jamie."

JUDY [*offering it*]. Want to finish my hamburger? I only took a bite.

PLATO. Okay. [*Accepts it.*]

[BUZZ *and* JIM *appear from out of darkness* D L *and move toward the lighted area.*]

BUZZ [*with approval, to* MOOSE]. You got some goodies for us. [*They pause a bit apart from group.*]

JIM. They look good.

MOOSE. Clean as a whistle. They both got plenty of breeze.

BUZZ. They look okay to you?

JIM. Sure. Fine.

BUZZ. Take your pick. Either one.

JIM. It doesn't make any difference.

BUZZ. What did you say your name was?

JIM. Jim Stark.

BUZZ. Buzz Gunderson.

JIM. Hi.

BUZZ. Glad to meet you. [*Shakes hands briefly.*] The doors are okay. I tested them. Remember, man, when you jump— quick. You gotta break quick.

JIM. Where do we start?

BUZZ. Over there. [*Gestures off* U L.] We head right for the cliff here. [*Gestures* D L, *looking around for a moment in almost lordly disdain.*]

JIM [*looking with him*]. We'll really give 'em a jolt. [*Nods toward others.*]

BUZZ [*quietly*]. This is the edge, boy. This is the end.

JIM. Yeah.

BUZZ. I like you, you know?

JIM [*after brief pause*]. Buzz, what are we doing this for?

BUZZ [*still quiet*]. We've got to do *something*, don't we?

JIM [*abruptly*]. Let's go. [BUZZ *crosses to* C, *where* JUDY *is standing with* PLATO.]

JUDY. Feel okay?

BUZZ. Give me some dirt. [JUDY *bends to ground, apparently picks up some dirt, and hands it to him. He rubs it into his palms. As he does this, he calls to* JIM.] Hey, Toreador! She signals. [*Nods toward* JUDY.] When she drops her sweater, we head for the edge. The first guy who jumps—chicken. [BUZZ *kisses* JUDY *dispassionately and briefly.*]

JUDY. Good luck, Buzz. [BUZZ *crosses* U L *and goes out.*]

JIM [*still standing at left edge of lighted area*]. Judy. [JUDY *crosses to him*]. Me, too. [JUDY *looks at him for a moment, then he holds out his hands for some dirt. She bends down and hands him some. Their hands touch and linger for a moment.*] Thank you. [JUDY *pulls her hands back hurriedly.*]

MOOSE [*crossing to* JIM]. You changed your mind? [JIM *looks at him contemptuously, turns without a word, and walks out* U L, *in direction* BUZZ *has taken.* MOOSE *speaks to* JUDY.] You stand out here where they can see you and give the starting signal. [*Sound of two cars starting up is heard off* U L.* *They gun their motors and then are heard pulling away. After they have gone a short distance, they can be heard distinctly in background revving up and then dying down and then revving up again.* MOOSE *and* CRUNCH *line up spectators in a line running from* U L *to* D L. *They all look off into darkness* U L, *where sound of two cars can be heard faintly.* JUDY *stands two steps in front of line with her sweater in her hand, held over her head. She swings it down in a wide sweeping gesture as starting signal. Suddenly cars can be heard rapidly accelerating and getting closer and louder.*]

MOOSE [*standing along edge of line of spectators*]. They're off!

PLATO [*to* JUDY]. Here they come!

JUDY [*staring in fascination, as do others*]. Yeah.

CRUNCH. Here they come!

GOON. They started slow.

---

*A special sound effects record is available incorporating all the police sirens, "chicken-run" automobile effects, and major sound effects required in this play.

HELEN. They have a ways to go yet.

MOOSE [*tight-lipped*]. Couple of seconds. [*During this dialogue, their eyes and heads turn as if following movements of a car which had progressed from off* U L *till they are looking directly off* D L.]

MILLIE [*from another spot in line, peering over*]. Someone better jump!

HELEN. I hope nothing goes wrong!

PLATO. There's Jim getting ready.

JUDY. He's got his door open.

CRUNCH [*with pride*]. Buzz is still in.

GOON [*yelling*]. Jump, man, jump!

MOOSE. He'd better.

GOON. Man, they're close!

MOOSE. I think there's something wrong.

PLATO. There goes Jim.

HELEN. He jumped!

MOOSE. They're at the cliff!

GOON. Buzz is still in there!

MILLIE. It's too late!

MOOSE. There go the cars! [JUDY *tenses and faces* D L, *as do others. There is a thunderous roar as cars go by and sounds start to fade away.* JUDY *gives a gasp that is almost a scream and puts her hands to her mouth. There is a long, shocked "oh" of horror and in-sucked breath as rest of spectators turn and face* D L. *We hear distant sound of a prolonged crash.*]

CRUNCH [*after a moment*]. His door was stuck. [MOOSE *and* CRUNCH *and others have walked to the* D L C *edge of stage and are looking down and over footlights as if over cliff. Several of the girls turn as if in horror. There is a long, dead silence.*]

MOOSE. He was trying to get out.

CRUNCH. He'll never know what hit him.

MOOSE. All the way down—he was the only man in the world.

[PLATO *has ducked out* D L.]

[*Now* PLATO *re-enters* D L, *supporting a dusty, disheveled* JIM.]

JIM. Where's Buzz? Where's Buzz?

CRUNCH [*from where he is standing, in tight fury, pointing over footlights*]. Down there, down there is Buzz! [JIM *looks at him blankly, then in dawning comprehension, walks over to edge,* D L C, *and looks over with him. After a moment, he turns away.*]

PLATO [*crossing to him*]. Come on, Jim. We should leave. [JIM *stands, paying no attention for a moment, then looks around till he spots* JUDY, *who is standing alone with her back to footlights.*]

JIM [*moving across toward her*]. I've got to talk to her.

PLATO. Best you leave her alone, Jim. [JIM *puts an arm around* JUDY'S *shoulder and leads her slowly* U C *in lighted area, half supporting her. When he comes to a spot near upper edge of light, he turns her around with one hand on each shoulder. After a moment, he pulls her closer and she buries her head on his chest, sobbing silently. During this action, spectators have slowly started to drift away, out* D L.]

JIM [*after a few moments*] Will you be okay? [JUDY *doesn't answer.*]

PLATO [*coming over to them*]. I got to go. We'd all better get out of here.

JIM [*looking down toward cliff, then back toward* PLATO]. Yeah.

PLATO. Everybody's gone.

JIM [*shrugging his downstage shoulder, nodding his head down toward* JUDY, *as if to say what can he do*]. I know.

PLATO. Why don't you both come home with me? I mean, nobody's home at my house—and I'm not tired. Are you? I don't have many people I can talk to.

JIM. Who has?

PLATO. If you want to come we could talk, and then in the morning we could have breakfast like my dad used to——

[*Pauses, then excitedly, as though an idea had suddenly struck him.*] Gee—if you could only have been my father, we could——

JIM [*interrupting*]. Hey, you flipped or something? You better take off.

PLATO [*suddenly, pleasantly*]. Okay, g'night. I got to pick up my scooter. See you tomorrow.

JIM. Yeah. [PLATO *turns and walks out* D L. JIM *gently takes a half step back from* JUDY.] We've got to go now. [JUDY *nods.*] It isn't safe for you to stay here. [*She nods again. He looks around and sees that stage is deserted.*] Come on, Judy. I'll take you home. [*They go out* D L, *slowly and silently. For a moment, stage is bare, and then, off in distance, approaching rapidly and getting louder, we hear distant sound of a police siren that grows to a loud, terrifying noise as* C *area light goes out.*]

[*A moment later, the lights come on at the* R *area. It is Jim's home, the same as before in this act.* MOTHER *is in a long, attractive housecoat and nightgown.* FATHER *is wearing the same clothes as when last seen, minus the apron.* MOTHER *is seated on the couch, sobbing.* FATHER *is sitting in the chair, pretending to be relaxed. Suddenly, from offstage* R, *there is the sound of a front door opening and closing. They both turn and sit up.*]

MOTHER. He's home. He's home!

FATHER. He's all right.

[JIM *appears* R *in the lighted area.*]

MOTHER [*as* JIM *appears in edge of lighted area*]. What happened, darling? We were so worried. I was going to take a sleeping pill, but I wouldn't till I knew you were home.

JIM [*obviously under great stress*]. I have to talk to someone, Mom. I have to talk to you both. And, Dad, this time you got to give me an answer. [*Pauses by table right of couch.*]

FATHER. Go ahead.

JIM. I'm in terrible trouble. You know that big high bluff near Millertown Junction?

FATHER. Sure. There was a bad accident there tonight. They showed the picture on T V.

JIM. I was in it.

MOTHER [*beginning to get hysterical again*]. How!

JIM. It doesn't matter now. I was driving a stolen car——

MOTHER. Do you *enjoy* doing this to me—or what?

JIM. Mom, I'm not——

MOTHER [*to* FATHER]. And you wanted him to make a *list!*

FATHER. Will you let him tell it!

JIM. She never wants to hear. She doesn't care!

MOTHER [*wave of self-pity*]. I guess when I nearly died giving birth to you—that shows how much I don't care!

FATHER. Just relax, please relax!

JIM. I told you, Dad, it was a question of honor. They called me chicken—you know, chicken! I had to go, or I would never have been able to face any of those kids again. So I got in one of those cars and a boy called Buzz got in the other. We had to drive fast and jump before the cars went over the edge of the bluff. I got out okay but Buzz didn't. He was killed.

MOTHER. Good Lord!

JIM. I can't keep it to myself any more.

FATHER. Well, just get it off your chest, son.

JIM [*moving behind couch and over to left of* FATHER *as he continues*]. That's not what I mean. I've never done anything right. I've been going around with my head in a sling for years. I don't want to drag you into this, but I can't help it. I don't think I can prove anything by going around pretending I'm tough any more, so maybe you look like one thing but you still feel like another.

FATHER. You're absolutely right!

JIM. Are you listening to me? You're involved in this! I want to go to the police and tell them I was mixed up in this thing tonight.

FATHER. You what?

MOTHER. No!

FATHER. Did anyone see you there? I mean, did they get your license number or anything?

JIM. I don't think so.

FATHER. Well——

MOTHER. What about the other boys? Do you think they'll go to the police?

JIM. What's that got to do with it?

MOTHER. Why should *you* be the only one?

FATHER [*rising*]. Look, Jim. Far be it from me to tell you what to do, but there's——

MOTHER. Are you going to preach now? Are we going to have a sermon?

FATHER [*to* MOTHER]. I'm just explaining what *you* mean! [*Turning back to* JIM.] You can't be an idealist all your life! Nobody thanks you for sticking your neck out.

MOTHER. That's right!

JIM. Except yourself!

FATHER. Will you wait a minute?

JIM. You don't want me to go.

MOTHER. No! I don't want you to go to the police! There were other people, and why should you be the only one involved?

JIM [*pacing* D R *in lighted area*]. But I *am* involved! We're all involved, Mom! A boy was *killed!* I don't see how we can get out of that by pretending it didn't happen!

FATHER. You know you did wrong. That's the main thing, isn't it?

JIM. No! It's nothing! Just nothing! You always told me to tell the truth. You think you can just turn that off?

MOTHER. He's not saying that! He's saying, "Don't volunteer!"

JIM [*contemptuously*]. Just tell a little white lie?

FATHER. You'll learn as you get a little older, Jim.

JIM. I don't want to learn that!

MOTHER. Well, it doesn't matter, anyhow—because we're moving.

JIM [*almost violently*]. No! You're not tearing me loose any more.

FATHER [*to* MOTHER]. This is news to me! Why are we moving?

MOTHER. Do I have to spell it out?

JIM. Yes, Mom. Maybe you'd better spell it out this time. Every time something goes wrong in the family, we have to move. Maybe it's my fault that things go wrong most of the time, but not *every* time. And maybe if just once, one person in this family faced up to something, maybe we wouldn't be in the messes we are. I don't care what you two do. I'm staying. [*Turns and looks at* FATHER.] Dad?

FATHER [*sinking into chair again*]. Son, this is all happening so fast——

JIM [*almost grimly*]. You better give me something, Dad. You better *give* me something fast. [*Stops as he sees emptiness in them.*] Mom?

MOTHER. Jimmy, you're very young, and a foolish decision now could wreck your whole life.

JIM. Dad—answer her—aren't you going to stand up for me? [FATHER *is mute, helpless. He turns away. Suddenly,* JIM *screams.*] Dad? [*Leaps at* FATHER, *dragging him to his feet, hands at* FATHER'S *throat.*]

MOTHER [*jumping up, moving toward them*]. Stop it! You'll kill him! Jim! Do you want to kill your father? [*Suddenly* JIM *loosens his hands. He looks swiftly at each of them, moves a few steps toward* R, *looks back at them again, then rushes out* R. MOTHER *and* FATHER *stand frozen. Lights go out.*]

[*The lights come on in the* C *area. We discover* RAY *and* GOON *seated in the chairs in the center of the stage. The scene is the police station, and the* L *area is also lit. In it we see* CRUNCH *waiting on the bench with the police* OFFICER *sitting behind the desk, writing up reports and occasionally eying* CRUNCH.]

RAY [*to* GOON]. You're a senior in high school. Your first name's Gordon but you're called Goon.

GOON. Man, you're right with it!

RAY. Do you drive a car? [GOON *gives him a disgusted look and slowly nods his head.*] You're a classmate of the Gunderson boy?

GOON. You mean Buzz. Yeah.

RAY. He's quite a wheel. You drive your own car?

GOON. It's in my dad's name. It's all legal.

RAY. The records say you were picked up for driving a stolen car two years ago. A judge put you on probation.

GOON. Some deal! I borrow a guy's car for a joyride and you yo-yo's have me figured for a hot car ring.

RAY. The owner was glad to get his car back. When did you last see Gunderson?

GOON [*quickly*]. In school. I saw him in school.

RAY. In one of your classes?

GOON. In the hallway.

RAY. After school? Or during school?

GOON. During school.

RAY. Is that the last time you saw him?

GOON. I just said so, daddy-o.

RAY. Do you know where the Millertown bluff is?

GOON. Yeah. [*With great display of innocence.*] I heard there was an accident.

RAY. When?

GOON. Ridin' around in the car with my friends. It was on the radio.

RAY. You heard what it was?

GOON. The word was—a chicken-run was on.

RAY. Who'd you get the word from?

GOON. I don't know. You hear these things. In the hall.

RAY. Someone must have told you.

GOON. In our school, you're lucky if you can hear what's said.

RAY. A chicken-run. That's quite a show.

GOON. So they say.

RAY. You want to give me the story?

GOON. I don't know anything about it.

RAY. We'll have five stories on this in the next two hours, signed statements from witnesses.

GOON. Daddy-o, it won't go. Can't tell you what I don't know.

RAY. *If* you don't know.

GOON. If information is so easy to get, why pick on me?

RAY. Somebody stole the cars that were used. You know how.

GOON. You going to try proving I stole a car?

RAY. No. [*Stands up and straightens out.*] You can go now.

GOON [*standing up and adjusting his belt with a swagger*]. You're gonna have a real interesting night, pop. I'm glad I could help. [*Begins to swagger toward* L *area.*]

RAY. That Buzz-man, he was quite a guy!

GOON [*off guard, pausing at left edge of* C *area*]. Buzz was the most. [*Looks back suddenly at* RAY, *aware of his slip, and then hoping that it hasn't been noted. He turns to go.*]

RAY. Wait a minute, son. [GOON *pauses.*] I want to tell you something. Did you ever shoot crap? Now you don't have to answer that question, but do you understand the game? [GOON *nods in affirmative in a rather bewildered way.*] Boy, every time you get in one of these scrapes—a ride in a stolen car, a street fight, maybe even if it's nothing illegal, or maybe something tragic like that chicken-run turned out to be, keep in mind that what you do is taking everything you've got in life—you family, your friends, your future, the chance for a marriage, a job, a happy life, every single thing —you're taking it and you're putting it on the line, and you're rolling the dice, and, son, you'd better pray you roll seven. You're playing with real high stakes. You can go home now. [GOON *looks at him for a moment, then turns without comment, and moves to right of bench in* L *area.* RAY *moves in front of desk in* L *area and speaks to* OFFICER.] This boy's free to go. I'll interview the next one.

OFFICER [*rising, leaning across with a small piece of paper*]. A message for you from headquarters. They want you downtown right away. They think they've got a——[*Catches himself.*] You want me to see what this punk knows? [*Nods toward* CRUNCH *on bench.*]

RAY. Yes, you'd better. I don't know how long I'll be. Take it easy.

OFFICER. Sure. [*Moves to bench.*] Come on, you. [*Nods with his head toward* C *area.* CRUNCH *rises, turns to* GOON, *who blows on his fingernails, and polishes them on his shirt.* RAY *goes out* D L.]

GOON [*sitting on bench*]. I'll wait for you.

CRUNCH. I'll drive you home. [*Follows* OFFICER *into the lighted* C *area and stands waiting.*]

OFFICER [*coming into* C *area*]. Sit down. [CRUNCH *sits in chair to right.* OFFICER *pulls other chair around by side of chair* CRUNCH *is sitting in, which faces downstage. He puts a foot on seat, leans forward with his forearm on his knee, and starts to question him.*] You know a fellow named Buzz Gunderson, don't you?

CRUNCH [*after a momentary pause*]. Yeah. I know him. He's in my class at school.

OFFICER. You pal around with him?

CRUNCH. No.

OFFICER. Our information is that you're one of his closest pals——

CRUNCH [*interrupting*]. Who could have told you a thing like that!

OFFICER [*continuing*]. —and you were seen with him at the Millertown bluff earlier this evening.

CRUNCH. Where they had the accident?

OFFICER. Don't give me back talk. Answers!

CRUNCH [*mockingly*]. Yes, sir! No, I was not at Millertown bluff and do not know what happened.

OFFICER. Who drove the other car?

CRUNCH [*a little bothered*]. I said I don't know.

OFFICER [*straightening up, with emphasis on each word*]. *We want to know who drove the other car.*

CRUNCH. I wasn't there.

OFFICER [*taking his foot off chair*]. I don't want smart talk. I want answers.

CRUNCH. I don't know a thing—not a thing.

OFFICER [*moving chair out from between him and boy*]. *Talk!*

CRUNCH [*controlling tightly what is almost hysterical fright*]. What's it gonna be—brass knuckles or a rubber hose?

OFFICER [*reaching down with both hands, grabbing* CRUNCH *by arms near shoulder, and pulling him sharply to his feet*]. Listen, punk, you'll be answering a lot of questions, and if you want to be a real hotshot, a *real* hero, better save it up for some information that's worth a quarter. For dime-store information, you don't prove nothing by talking smart except that you're a punk who's gonna be back for more. Go home. [*Shoves him toward the lighted area* L.] Remember one thing, son. You're safe. All we wanted was information. But listen. Don't ever get caught doing anything you shouldn't. [*There is a pause. He nods* D L.] Get! [CRUNCH *jerks away and almost starts to run out, remembers himself, stops, realizes that he has held out, and slowly swaggers from the lighted area* C *into lighted area* L. OFFICER *follows. As they enter* L *area*, GOON, *who has been seated on bench, rises.*]

[*At this moment*, JIM *enters* D L. *He stops and looks at them without saying anything. They look at him.* JIM *crosses to the desk and waits in front of it. The* OFFICER *speaks to* GOON *and* CRUNCH.]

OFFICER. You can go now. [CRUNCH *and* GOON *look at each other, then at* JIM.]

CRUNCH [*to* JIM]. This place appeal to you or somethin'?

OFFICER. You know this guy?

CRUNCH. No, and don't want to. Anybody who'd walk in here of his own free will——[*Stops suddenly.*] Come on, Goon.

[CRUNCH *and* GOON *go quickly out* D L. JIM *glances after them and then turns back to* OFFICER, *who has seated himself behind desk. Telephone rings, and* JIM *sits down on bench.*]

OFFICER [*into telephone*]. Sergeant Mullen. Just a moment, please. [*Puts receiver down and looks at* JIM.] Yes?

JIM. Excuse me, but—you know where I can find—I mean, I don't remember his last name——

OFFICER. I'll be right with you. [*Into telephone.*] Hello? . . . No. . . . *No.* Hold on a second. [*Looks up.*] Yes?

JIM. I think his first name is Ray. I have to see him. It's very important.

OFFICER. He's not here now. He left a little while ago and won't be back. I'll take care of you. Just a minute. [*Into telephone.*] Can I call you back? . . . Well, then hang on a minute more while I take care of this. [*Puts telephone down.*] All right. Now, what's it about?

JIM. I just wanted to see this officer. His name is Ray.

OFFICER. I explained that he won't be in until later. I'll be glad to take care of you. Do you have a complaint?

JIM. No.

OFFICER [*with a flash of interest*]. Do you know anything about this accident at Millertown bluff? We'll be glad to take a statement.

JIM [*rising, moving* D L]. It was a personal thing. I wanted to see Ray.

OFFICER. Well, he won't be back until very much later. Why don't you come back tomorrow, son? He's having a pretty busy evening. [JIM *shrugs, looks out* D L, *where* GOON *and* CRUNCH *have gone out, then back to* OFFICER.]

JIM. Well, I'll try and make it. [OFFICER *picks up telephone and* JIM *starts out* D L *as lights go out on both* C *and* L *areas.*]

[*The light comes on in the* c *area again a few moments later. The area is clear.* BELLE *is seen catching up with* JUDY, *at* c. *Both have entered from* U R *stage.*]

BELLE. Judy. Judy! Wait a minute. [JUDY *turns and faces her as* BELLE *runs up to her.*] What are you doing outside this way? Why didn't you stay home?

JUDY. I don't know, Belle. I'm jumpy tonight. You know what dinner was. When I came home, the house was dark. Nobody said a word. I'm upset. I couldn't stand it. I had to get out.

BELLE. You shouldn't be out on the street at night. You remember the last time.

JUDY. Yes. I remember.

BELLE. There was a phone call. Some guy I didn't know. His name was Jim. He was real disappointed when I told him you were out.

JUDY. Come on. I'll walk you home.

[PLATO *appears out of the darkness* D R.]

PLATO [*to* JUDY, *as he comes into* c *area*]. Judy!

JUDY. Hi, Plato.

PLATO. Can I talk to you a minute?

JUDY. Sure. Belle, you go ahead. I'll catch up with you. [BELLE *looks at the two of them for a moment, looks* PLATO *up and down, and shakes her head negatively.*]

BELLE [*to* JUDY]. Don't forget that phone call. That sounded very interesting to me. [*Looks at* PLATO *with some disdain and then goes off into the darkness* U R.]

PLATO [*as soon as* BELLE *leaves*]. They're looking for him.

JUDY. What's up?

PLATO. I don't know, but they're looking for him. Crunch came to my house and asked me where Jim was. I didn't know. He wanted me to come out with him. I wouldn't go.

JUDY. Why? What's up?

PLATO. I don't know. But it's bad. I went around to Jim's house to try to tell him. Somebody nailed a dead chicken to his front door.

[*Out of the darkness* U R, CRUNCH, MOOSE, *and* GOON *appear. They stand there silently for a moment.* PLATO, *hearing them come, turns quickly.*]

PLATO. What do you want?

CRUNCH [*as three boys come into* C *area*]. You know what we want. We want your friend.

GOON. We got eyes for him.

PLATO. Listen, you guys ought to go home. The cops are cruising everywhere.

GOON [*breaking in*]. Where is he?

PLATO. He's at home.

CRUNCH. Don't give us that. We've been there.

PLATO [*edging toward left of* C *area as boys close in on him*]. I don't know where he is.

CRUNCH. You better tell. I'm not kidding.

PLATO. Don't come near me. I've got a gun!

MOOSE. Now that's really something! He's got a gun. [*Hits* PLATO *a hard blow in belly with his fist.*]

MOOSE. Your friend talked.

GOON [*hitting him again*]. Now you talk. Talk!

[MRS. DAVIS *appears* D R.]

MRS. DAVIS [*coming into* C *area*]. What are you doin'? What are you doin' to that boy? [*Boys stop.* PLATO *is standing, but doubled over, holding his stomach.*] You clear out of here before I call the police. Clear out! Go on! Go on now!

JUDY [*to boys*]. He doesn't know anything. I was talking to him just before.

MOOSE. Let's go. [MOOSE, CRUNCH, *and* GOON *start* D L, *and go out* D L. PLATO, *after a moment's hesitation, takes a gun out of his pocket and takes a half step after them.*]

MRS. DAVIS [*grabbing him*]. John, what are you doin' with that? You put that down! Put it down before you hurt yourself! [PLATO *shakes his head and then lowers his arm with gun in it.*] Why you like to mix with bad boys like that? Why you get in trouble all the time?

PLATO. I have to find Jim. I have to warn him.

JUDY. I'll help.

MRS. DAVIS. I'm goin' home now, John, and telephone your mother by long distance. [*Starts* D R.] You're in trouble—bad trouble.

PLATO. I've got to warn him. [MRS. DAVIS *goes out* D R. PLATO *calls after her.*] Mrs. Davis, don't call my mother. Listen, I'll explain. [*Runs* D R *and goes out after her.*]

[JIM *appears* U L.]

JIM [*pausing* U L; JUDY'S *back is to him*]. Judy.

JUDY [*whirling around with a gasp*]. Jim!

JIM [*hurrying to her*]. I've been looking for you. I had to talk to you. I phoned, but you weren't home.

JUDY. I know. They're looking for you.

JIM. They saw where I jumped. I didn't chicken. What do I have to do—kill myself?

JUDY. It doesn't matter to them.

JIM. They saw me come into the police station.

JUDY. So that's it. You'd better be careful, Jim. They'll kill you. I'm serious.

JIM. Were you looking for me?

JUDY. I was just—[*Pauses.*]—well—[*In a small voice.*]—maybe.

JIM. You still pretty upset?

JUDY. I'm numb. [*Shudders a little.*]

JIM. You cold? [*Takes her arm.*]

JUDY. Even if I'm near a fire, I'm cold. I guess just about everybody's cold.

JIM. I swear, sometimes, you just want to hold onto somebody! Judy, what am I going to do? I can't go home again.

JUDY. You can't! Why?

JIM. Mainly because they'll be watching for me.

JUDY. You're right to be careful, but that isn't what you were talking about.

JIM. Home isn't a place—it's a state of mind—a relationship between people. You always think it's a place till something goes wrong, and you suddenly realize you haven't got a home.

JUDY. What happened?

JIM. It's too long a story.

JUDY. I can't go home, either.

JIM. No? Why not? [*No answer.*] You know something? Sometimes I figure I'll never live to see my next birthday. Isn't that dumb?

JUDY. No.

JIM. Every day I look in the mirror and say, "What? You still here?" Man! [*They laugh a little.*] Hey! You smiled! [*JUDY shakes her head, beginning to warm to him.*] Like even today. I woke up this morning, you know? And the sun was shining and everything was nice. Then the first thing that happens is I see you, and I thought this is going to be one terrific day so you better live it up, boy, 'cause tomorrow maybe you'll be nothing.

JUDY. I'm sorry I treated you mean today. You shouldn't believe what I say when I'm with the kids. Nobody acts sincere.

JIM. Why'd you get mixed up with them? You don't have to prove anything.

JUDY [*moving a little away from him*]. If you knew me you wouldn't say that.

JIM. I don't think you trust anybody, do you?

JUDY. Why?

JIM. I'm getting that way, too.

JUDY [*looking at him*]. Have *you* ever gone with anyone who——

JIM [*moving toward her again*]. Sure. Lots of times.

JUDY. So have I. But I've never been in love. Isn't that awful?

JIM [*smiling*]. Awful? No It's just lonely. It's the loneliest
time. [JUDY *looks up. He kisses her forehead.*]

JUDY. Why did you do that?

JIM. I felt like it.

JUDY. Your lips are soft when you kiss. [*Moves away from
him, right.*]

JIM. Where you going?

JUDY. I don't know, but we can't stay here.

JIM [*moving after her*]. Where can we go? I can't go back
into the zoo.

JUDY. I'm never going back.

JIM. Listen! I know a place! Plato showed me. An old deserted
mansion near the planetarium. Would you go with me?
[JUDY *hesitates.*] You can trust me, Judy.

JUDY. I feel as if I'm walking under water. [JIM *takes her arm
and they start out* D R.]

CURTAIN

ACT THREE

[*It is still later the same evening. The scene is the police station, the* L *lighted area. The* OFFICER *is seated behind his desk.* MRS. DAVIS *is seated on the bench on the far right-hand side. She sits quietly with her hands folded in her lap throughout.* RAY *is standing in front of the desk, talking to Mr. and Mrs. Stark,* MOTHER *and* FATHER, *who are right of him.*]

MOTHER. It's been perfectly horrible!

FATHER [*abruptly*]. We're not here about that.

RAY. You want your son.

FATHER. Yes. I don't know what's going on.

MOTHER. Apparently one of his—escapades—has gotten him in trouble with some of his contemporaries.

FATHER. He's in trouble. I think he needs help.

OFFICER [*from desk*]. You say you found a dead chicken nailed to the outside of your front door?

MOTHER [*shuddering*]. Horrid!

RAY. It's supposed to mean something.

FATHER. I know. Chicken. Coward. Maybe they put it on the right door.

MOTHER. How can you criticize at a time like this!

FATHER. I wasn't talking about Jim.

MOTHER. That wasn't all, Officer. When I got outside the door, some kids were in the bushes. They shouted questions at me.

RAY. What questions?

FATHER. They wanted to know where Jim was.

MOTHER. Depraved—that's what they are!

FATHER. No—just teen-agers.

OFFICER. What'd they say?

FATHER. "Where's your baby boy? We want him. Tell the chicken to come out."

RAY. I'm afraid there's nothing I can do.

MOTHER. What do you mean?

RAY. There's a rumble on. Parents don't usually know, but tonight is different. We've heard from a number of parents. [*Looks at* OFFICER, *who looks back.*]

OFFICER. All squads have been alerted to look out for any assembly or unusual activity on the part of teen-agers. [*Telephone rings on desk.* OFFICER *picks it up with his left hand, writing on a pad with his right hand.*] Sergeant Mullen. . . . Yeah—you mean that old deserted mansion? . . . By the planetarium—yeah. . . . Got it. Okay. Thanks. [*Hangs up and turns to* RAY.] We have a report from a squad car saying that a jalopy, a heap, and a motor scooter are parked outside the old mansion out on Summit Drive by the planetarium. There's also a broken window on the ground floor of the mansion.

RAY. Sounds like my department.

OFFICER. Yeah—those darling teen-age cut-ups.

RAY. I'll take a car and investigate. [*Turns to* FATHER.] Want to come?

MOTHER. Do you think it's Jim?

RAY [*shaking his head*]. Probably not, but it'll be easier than waiting—like her. [*Nods to* MRS. DAVIS.]

MRS. DAVIS [*looking up*]. Please, sir, can I come, too?

RAY. Sure—come along if you wish. Nothing will happen—you know that.

MRS. DAVIS [*crossing toward others*]. I'd like to come, if you don't mind. [*Directs this to* MOTHER *and* FATHER.]

MOTHER. By all means. It must be deadly waiting around here. [*Gives a delicate shudder.*]

MRS. DAVIS. My boy, John, he been up to that old house before. [*Pauses.*] Something awful gonna happen.

RAY [*gently*]. There must be some reason, Mrs. Davis. If you'd only tell me.

MRS. DAVIS. Ain't got no reason.

RAY. All right. Come along. The car's in back. [*Turns to OF-FICER.*] I'll keep in touch by radio in case anything comes in on your side. [*Goes out* D L *with* MOTHER, FATHER, *and* MRS. DAVIS. *Lights go out.*]

[*The stage is dark for a brief period. After a moment of silence, we hear* JUDY.]

JUDY [U C]. Jim! It's so dark. [*After* JUDY'S *speech, a flashlight is turned on at* U C, *and lights* C *fade in slowly but dimly, not too bright.* JIM, U C, *is carrying a flashlight lantern.*]

JIM. I had this flashlight lantern in the trunk of my car. I didn't want to turn it on outside in case somebody saw us breaking in. [*Swings lantern around, following arc of proscenium. Both* JIM *and* JUDY *are approaching* C *from* U C.]

JUDY [*looking up and following light*]. I never saw a building with pictures on the ceiling before.

JIM. You can't see much. It's so dusty.

JUDY [*as* JIM *brings light back down and slowly lets it traverse from right to left, out over heads of audience*]. Crazy! Statues, too.

JIM. The place is certainly a mess.

JUDY. We're safe here. [*From offstage* R, PLATO *calls out.*]

PLATO [*offstage* R]. Jim!

JIM [*turning suddenly with* JUDY *in direction of sound, dousing flashlight*]. Who's that? [C *light has gone out.*]

PLATO [*offstage* R]. It's me—Plato.

JIM [*turning on flashlight*]. Come on in. [*Light* C *comes on again, as before.*]

PLATO [*offstage* R]. Be with you in a second.

JIM. How did you find me? What's happening?

[PLATO *appears in the* C *area from* R.]

PLATO. They're looking for you.

JIM. Yeah?

PLATO. Everybody! Crunch and Goon and everybody! I think they're going to kill you.

JIM. We know.

PLATO. They think you told the police on them. They——— [*Realizes someone is in room with them and stops suddenly.*] Who's there?

JIM. Judy.

JUDY [*advancing a step halfway into light*]. Hi, Plato.

PLATO. You sure no one saw you?

JUDY. I came with Jim.

PLATO. You're okay then. Ever been here before?

JUDY. No. What is it, anyway? I can't see anything, but things sound funny here.

PLATO. It's a crazy mansion with statues and paintings on the wall—crazy.

JIM. We're safe, I hope.

PLATO. They'll never find us here.

JIM. I hope not. I'm scared. [*Flashes his light so he can see sort of place he is in.*]

PLATO. What do you think? Isn't it crazy?

JIM. Wow-ee! Let's take it for the summer.

JUDY. Oh, Jim!

JIM. No, come on. Should we rent or are we in a buying mood, dear?

JUDY [*laughing, taking his arm*]. You decide, darling. Remember our budget.

PLATO [*joining in the game*]. Don't give it a thought. Only three million dollars a month!

JUDY. Oh, we can manage that! I'll scrimp and save and work my fingers to the bone. . . .

JIM. Why don't we just rent it for the season?

JUDY. You see, we've just———Oh, *you* tell him, darling. I'm so embarrassed I could die! [*Hides her head on* JIM'S *shoulder in mock shyness.*]

JIM. Well, we're newlyweds.

JUDY. There's just one thing. What about———

PLATO. Children? Well, we really don't encourage them. They're so noisy and troublesome, don't you agree?

JUDY. Yes, and so terribly annoying when they cry. I just don't know what to do when they cry, do you, dear?

JIM. Of course. Drown them like puppies.

JUDY. See, we're very modern.

PLATO. Shall I show you the nursery? [*Moves a few steps right.*] It's far away from the rest of the house. If you have children—oh, I hate the word!—or if you decide to adopt one—they can carry on and you'll never even notice. In fact, if you lock them in you never have to see them again, much less talk to them. [*Moves R C, as JUDY and JIM follow. Light moves with them.*]

JUDY [*mock horror*]. *Talk* to them! Heavens!

JIM. Nobody *talks* to children! They just tell them one thing and mean another.

PLATO. It's wonderful that you understand so well—and so young, too! You know the most wonderful feature about the nursery?

JIM. What?

PLATO. There's only one key.

JIM. We'll take it!

PLATO. Come on!

JIM. I specially like the furniture.

JUDY [*looking about*]. But there isn't any furniture.

PLATO [*breaking playful mood*]. Man, you're schizoid!

JUDY [*laughing*]. He's what? What?

JIM. We might as well sit down. [*Waves his hand as if inviting them to be seated on an imaginary sofa; to PLATO.*] May I offer you a chair? [*To JUDY.*] You might like this straight-back chair. As for me, I'll sit on the piano stool. [*With this, he sits on floor at R C.*]

PLATO [*to JUDY*]. Isn't he schizoid?

JIM. There he goes again. [*All laugh cheerfully.*]

PLATO. Haven't you noticed your personality splitting?

JIM. Not lately.

JUDY [*who has been wandering around* U R C]. Here's an old
blanket I found. [*Spreads blanket at* R C *and then sinks
down onto blanket.*]

JIM. How do you know so much about this junk, Plato?

PLATO. I had to go to a head-shrinker. I only went twice,
though. My mother said it cost too much, so she went to
Hawaii instead. [*All three distribute themselves on blanket,
so that* JUDY *is seated on left side.* JIM *is in the middle with
his feet pointed* D R *and his head in* JUDY'S *lap.* PLATO *sits
quite near, to the right of them, knees up, chin resting on
knees.*]

JIM. No, seriously. What's your trouble?

PLATO [*hesitating a moment, then leaning back on one elbow*].
I don't know, but whatever it is, it's gone now. I mean, I'm
happy now. Here. I came here before.

JIM. When was that?

PLATO. When I was here? When I ran away. I used to run
away a lot but they always took me back.

JIM. Who?

PLATO. Mom and Dad. I used to be in my crib and I'd listen
to them fight.

JIM. You remember that far back? Boy, I can't even remember
yesterday.

JUDY. Plato, where's your father now?

PLATO [*quickly, obviously making it up*]. He's dead. He was
a hero in the China Sea.

JIM. You told me he's a big wheel in New York!

PLATO. I did? Well, he might as well be dead. What's the difference?

JUDY. It's all right.

JIM. Sure.

PLATO [*after brief pause*]. Man, this is peaceful.

JIM. Yeah. It's quiet. [*During above two speeches,* JUDY *has
softly begun to hum to herself and stroke* JIM'S *forehead
with her hand.* PLATO *has gradually straightened out his legs
and is stretched out on floor.*]

PLATO. I'm real tired. [*Goes to sleep.* JUDY *looks over at him and continues to hum, putting a finger to her lips to indicate to* JIM *that he should be quiet as* PLATO *is going to sleep.* JIM *half raises his head from her lap, turns to look, and then relaxes. As she starts to stroke his head again, he takes her hand and kisses it.*]

JIM [*looking at palm of her hand*]. You have a long lifeline.

JUDY [*taking his palm and examining it*]. So have you. [*Kisses his hand, holds her cheek against it.*]

JIM. Ever been in a place like this before?

JUDY. Not exactly. It's certainly huge.

JIM. How many rooms do you think there are?

JUDY. I don't know.

JIM. Should we explore? [JUDY *looks at* PLATO. JIM *shrugs.*]

JUDY [*very softly, to see if he is awake*]. Plato—Plato. [*There is no response from the sleeping* PLATO.] He's asleep.

JIM. That's funny—being able to drop off to sleep like that. I wish I could. [*They carefully get up, being careful not to disturb* PLATO. *After they are up,* JIM *takes part of blanket they have been on and puts it over* PLATO *with great gentleness.* JUDY *tucks* PLATO *in from other side, bends down, kisses his cheek softly, and then rises.* JIM *offers her his arm and nods to flashlight, which is still burning on floor by* PLATO.] I think you'll find it more romantic by moonlight. [*They walk* L, *holding hands, and then wander off into area* D L, *in which the lights come on softly.* JIM *looks around.*] Isn't this the craziest?

JUDY. Hi.

JIM. Hi. [*Pauses.*] What?

JUDY. Your hand's all wet and it's shaky. You're so funny.

JIM. Why?

JUDY. I don't know—you just are. Leaving a light for Plato. That was nice.

JIM. Maybe he's scared of the dark.

JUDY. Are you? [*A pause.*]

JIM [*singing*]. Here we are—out of cigarettes—

Junior's in the nurs'ry—
See how late it gets—

JUDY [*seriously*]. You don't need to do that.

JIM. There's something I should tell you, Judy.

JUDY. I know already. We don't have to pretend now.

JIM [*laughing*]. What a relief! [JUDY *snuggles close to him, her head on his shoulder. Both are gazing front, over heads of audience.*]

JUDY. Is this what it's like to love somebody?

JIM. You disappointed?

JUDY [*mussing his hair*]. Funny Jimmy. You're so clean and you——This is silly.

JIM. What?

JUDY. You smell like baby powder. [*Laughs rather foolishly.*]

JIM. So do you.

JUDY. I never felt so clean before.

JIM. It's not going to be lonely, Judy. Not for you and not for me.

JUDY [*almost lyrically*]. *I love somebody.* All this time I've been looking for someone to love me, and now—I love somebody. And it's so easy. Why is it easy now?

JIM. It is for me, too.

JUDY [*turning to him*]. I love you, Jim. I really mean it. [*Kisses his lips gently and looks into his face. He returns kiss. Their arms go around each other.*]

JIM. You change things.

JUDY. How?

JIM. A lot of the time I just don't care.

JUDY. You mean at home?

JIM. Yes—I feel I have to get out—break away.

JUDY. I know.

JIM. That talk—when we were kidding about a home.

JUDY. Not just kidding.

JIM. Maybe I've been confusing growing away from my folks with growing up.

JUDY. There's a point where your folks can't help you any more——

JIM. They could—[*He is bitter.*]—they just won't.

JUDY. I don't know, but I don't think it's their fault, either.

JIM. Sometimes at home I feel like a tiger in a cage—I'm well fed—I got everything, but it isn't natural to stay there. I've got to get out. I've got to escape.

JUDY. That must be hard on your folks.

JIM [*good-humoredly*]. It'd make me nervous.

JUDY. And now?

JIM. Well, now, maybe I know what I want to do, or at least where to go from here.

JUDY. It's easier for me. I just needed someone to love. I love you, Jim. I mean it.

JIM. I mean it, too. Come on. We've got to explore the rest of this place. [*They pass through dimly lighted area* D L *and out* D L. *Light* D L *goes out. Stage is left with area* R C *lighted with the sleeping* PLATO.]

[*After a brief pause, three flashlights come from the area* U R. *They flash around, making a pattern as the source of each light gradually approaches the sleeping* PLATO. *One of them catches him, and the other two quickly follow. They quickly converge on him so that one is directly right of him, one directly to the left, and one is upstage of him. They are* CRUNCH, MOOSE, *and* GOON.]

CRUNCH [*upstage of* PLATO]. This character turns up everywhere!

MOOSE [*right of* PLATO]. He's around. Wherever this Joe is, the other's around. Come on.

GOON [*left of* PLATO]. Maybe if we played some soft music, he'd hear us. [*Clinks a chain in his hands.*] This old dump —I don't like walking around in here.

CRUNCH. Tire chain music. [*They all edge slightly closer around* PLATO. *As they move,* PLATO, *who has been awake but pretending to be asleep, suddenly darts between*

CRUNCH *and* GOON, *toward* U L. *As he starts to scramble to his feet and away,* CRUNCH *grabs him.*]

PLATO. Jim! Jim! Save me!

CRUNCH. Good morning, Plato.

GOON [*clinking chain in his hand*]. I feel a real kick comin' on.

PLATO. You're crowding me too close—I'm warning you.

CRUNCH [*kicking flashlight lantern offstage* R; *lights dim*]. We don't want to crowd you. We'll move back—Goon, take that door—[*Points* L.]—Moose—that one. [*Points* U C.] I'll take the window. [*Backs toward* R, *as* GOON *moves* L, MOOSE U C. PLATO, *realizing they are covering all exits, pauses irresolutely at* C *stage for a moment, but before others have completed their movements he makes a sudden dash toward darkness* U C *where* MOOSE *has gone. There is a thud, a grunt, and* PLATO *staggers back to* R C, *clutching his stomach where he has been hit. He looks around desperately, looking for an exit, and sees from each section the flashlight pointing at him and from the dark the dim figures of the three boys.*]

PLATO. You better leave me alone! [*Starts to walk toward* R. CRUNCH *gives a loud animal grunt, and takes a heavy-footed step toward* PLATO. PLATO *stops, starts to edge toward* U C. *He stops and then starts to edge* L *into darkness. There is another grunt and sound of two heavy-footed steps advancing.* PLATO *stops, looks around, and begins to edge toward* U L.]

GOON [*from darkness* U L]. That's my baby, come to papa. He has something to put you to sleep with—a nice soft tire chain. [*Jumps a step toward* PLATO, *landing loudly with feet together.*]

PLATO [*coming back* C]. Let me alone—I tell you—let me alone. [*Now* CRUNCH *advances a step and grunts. They are playing cat and mouse, enjoying* PLATO'S *hysterical fear.* MOOSE *also moves a step closer and grunts.* PLATO, *seeing no way out from three advancing lights, begins slowly to back toward footlights.*]

PLATO. I'm warning you—leave me alone.

CRUNCH. Man, you're really gonna be alone.

MOOSE. And far out. [*Three boys continue to advance.* PLATO *suddenly darts toward* CRUNCH *and there is another thud. A moment later, he reels back, clutching his face. The lights start to close in on him again and he continues to back toward footlights.* MOOSE *takes a step and speaks to others.*] Come on. Let's make it.

PLATO [*almost to edge of footlights now*]. Stay away from me. I've got a gun!

GOON [*clinking chain in his hand*]. This is the craziest! [*Starts forward with chain in his hand, ready to strike.* PLATO *looks around desperately at other two, then draws his gun and fires in dark at* GOON. *There is a shocked gasp for breath;* GOON'S *flashlight falls, and then there is a groan and* PLATO *dashes* D L. *As he leaves the* C *area, flashlights go off.*]

[PLATO *runs into area* D L, *where lights come on and where he sees* JIM, *who has appeared from offstage* D L.]

PLATO [*almost shrieking*]. What do you run out on me for? What do you leave me alone for? [JIM *tries to pacify him.* PLATO *backs away.*] I don't want you for my father!

JIM. Your father? [PLATO *fires at* JIM. JIM *leaps forward and grabs* PLATO *from side with one arm around him and other holding gun arm out.*] You crazy nut! You crazy, crazy, nut!

PLATO [*screaming*]. Get away from me! [*Breaks loose from* JIM *and bolts off toward* C *and into darkness, offstage* U R. *There is sound of two shots.*]

[*As the sound of the two shots is heard in the distance,* JUDY *comes in* D L.]

JUDY. What happened?

JIM. Plato has a gun. Somebody must have frightened him.

JUDY. You mean he shot somebody?

JIM. I don't know—he shot at me.

JUDY. Oh, no, Jim! Did he hit you? [*She is on verge of hysteria.*]

JIM. No!

JUDY. We have to get out of here. [*Starts out* D L.]

JIM. No! I got to find Plato.

JUDY [*who has turned back*]. After he tried to shoot you?

JIM. He didn't mean it—we shouldn't have left him. He needed us.

JUDY. He needed you, maybe. So do I. [*There is sound of another shot in distance, offstage* U R.]

JIM. He needs you, too. Come on. [JUDY *starts after him as he crosses toward* C.]

JUDY. You should have heard him talk about you tonight. Like you were the hero in the China Seas.

JIM. Sure. He was trying to make us his family.

JUDY. They're killing him! [*They both start to run out* U R. *Lights go off* D L.]

[*A moment later the lights come up on* R *where we find* RAY *and two* POLICE OFFICERS, *with* FATHER, MOTHER, *and* MRS. DAVIS *standing in the background. Extras may be included as a crowd at this point if desired. They should stand a step or two behind* FATHER *and* MOTHER, *and* MRS. DAVIS. *Additional policemen can also be included.*]

OFFICER ONE [*pointing off* D R]. There he goes—into the planetarium!

OFFICER TWO. He broke the glass door with the butt of his gun. [*Shakes his head.*] A real nut.

RAY. You better get on the car radio—[*Nods toward area immediately offstage* R.]—and notify them to send the nearest car to cover the back door to this place.

OFFICER ONE. We better keep an eye on the old mansion where he came from [*Nods toward* L.]

OFFICER TWO. That's a real cuckaboo. [OFFICER ONE *goes out* R. OFFICER TWO *turns to* RAY.] I don't like being shot at.

RAY. That figures.

MRS. DAVIS [*advancing to* RAY'S *side*]. What you goin' to do?

RAY. We've got to round up these kids before they hurt somebody.

MRS. DAVIS. My boy—when he run off he had a gun with him.

RAY. Plato—he's called Plato—isn't he?

MRS. DAVIS. Yes, sir. You saw him, sir, about the puppies.

RAY. Could that have been him running from that old mansion into the planetarium?

MRS. DAVIS. I can't tell, sir—it's too far to see his face clearly. He's been here before.

RAY. It'd help if I knew. Sometimes I can talk to kids. A loaded gun makes it dangerous.

MRS. DAVIS. John, he's a real nice boy—he's not well. He can't help it. You won't hurt him?

RAY [*speaking carefully*]. That's what I'm here for—to help him. I'll do my best.

[OFFICER ONE *appears from* R.]

RAY [*turning to him*]. How long a wait?

OFFICER ONE. They're pulling around in back now. They had cars on the way. They'd been getting reports of the shooting.

RAY. You got a P.A. in that car?

OFFICER ONE. Yes. [RAY *goes out* R.]

OFFICER TWO [*who has been looking out* R]. Watch out! Here comes another bunch.

OFFICER ONE [*looking out* R]. There are just two—a boy and a girl.

OFFICER TWO. Headed for the planetarium—after the cuckaboo. What do you suppose is going on? Crazy kids running from a deserted mansion with nothing in it but junk to a planetarium with nothing in it but chairs and lights on the ceiling.

FATHER [*to* MOTHER]. That's Jim!

MOTHER. You can't tell from this distance. It's just the jacket he's wearing.

FATHER. I know my boy.

[RAY *enters* R *on this line with a microphone in his hand and crosses over to the* POLICE OFFICERS.]

FATHER. Stay here. [*Follows* RAY *and speaks to him.*] That was my son.

RAY [*turning to him*]. You sure? [*A siren is heard approaching, offstage* R.]

FATHER. I think I know my own son.

RAY. All right. [*Over P.A. speaker.*] Jim Stark! I'm addressing Jim Stark. Nobody will harm you or your friends if you follow these instructions. We are here to protect you. Drop your guns and come outside. Nobody will hurt you if you do as I say——

OFFICER TWO [*pointing off* L]. Looks like we're getting some from both buildings. There come three out of the old mansion. [*Turns to* RAY.] Well, you flushed some game!

OFFICER ONE. Looks like one of them has hurt his arm. That boy with a gun is dangerous. Go bring those other three in.

RAY. Have the doctor treat the boy's arm right away. [*Siren is heard approaching closer.* OFFICER TWO *goes into darkness and out* L. RAY *puts microphone just offstage* R *a moment.*] Keep the crowd back. Get some of those officers to hold the crowd back. We're getting too many people. The ones here —[*Nods to* FATHER *and* MOTHER *and* MRS. DAVIS.]—can stay. [*Lights* R *go off.*]

[*The light in the* C *area comes on again softly. The noises of the crowd are still heard, but more softly, as if farther off. An additional siren offstage* R *heralds the approach of another police car. The scene is in the planetarium, but the stage is bare.*]

JIM [*offstage* U R C, *heard from just outside area of sound, calling softly*]. Plato. [*There is a silence. Nothing moves.* JIM *calls again.*] Plato. You in there? [*There is a moment more of silence.*] Plato. I'm going to step in where you can see me. You can shoot me if you want to, but just remember one thing—you're my friend. That means a lot to me. [*Steps into lighted area from* U R C. *There is no sound for a moment.* JIM *calls again.*] Plato?

PLATO [*in darkness* U L C]. I'm here.

JIM [*his hand out gropingly*]. Boy, I'm blind as a bat! I'm going to break my neck in here. Where are you?

PLATO. I've got a gun.

JIM. I know. Come in where I can see you. [PLATO *comes a little closer, but still cannot be seen.*] That's swell. How are you?

PLATO. I'm fine.

JIM. Here we are in this crazy planetarium again.

PLATO. It seems like a long time ago.

JIM. You feel all right, Plato?

PLATO. You think the end of the world will come at night time, Jim?

JIM. No. At dawn.

PLATO. Why?

JIM. I just have a feeling. Where are you?

PLATO. Here.

JIM. Well, stop hiding and come in where I can see you. I can't talk to you if I don't see you. [PLATO *slowly steps halfway into lighted area so that at least the lower portion of his body is visible.*] That's fine. I'm not going to hurt you.

PLATO [*like a child*]. Why did you run out on me?

JIM. We didn't run out. We were coming right back.

PLATO. You sure?

JIM. Sure, I'm sure. Judy's waiting. You ready to come out now? [*Siren is heard offstage* R.]

PLATO. No.

JIM. I promise nothing'll happen if you do. [*Silence.*] You want my jacket? It's warm. [*Takes off his jacket and holds it out to* PLATO.]

PLATO [*stepping forward into light to meet* JIM]. Can I keep it?

JIM. What do *you* think? [*Gives him jacket, and* PLATO *puts it on.*] You want to give me your gun now, Plato?

PLATO [*almost defensively*]. My gun?

JIM. In your pocket. Give it to me.

PLATO [*drawing back slightly*]. I need it.

JIM. You trust me, don't you? Just give it to me for a second. [*Holds out his hand.*]

PLATO [*backing away*]. I can't.

JIM [*standing still, his hand still extended*]. It's dangerous, Plato.

PLATO. I know—that's why I need it. They were going to stomp me.

JIM. They're probably still running. They aren't here in the planetarium.

PLATO. You're not my friend. You left me when they were going to beat me—one of them had a tire chain.

JIM. They're gone now and I'm right here—we've got friends outside.

PLATO [*backing away another step*]. I haven't got any friends. That's why I need my gun.

JIM [*still not moving*]. *I'm* your friend, Plato. I'll walk out with you—we'll go together.

PLATO. You won't let them do anything?

JIM. We'll be okay, Plato, as long as you don't use the gun. There are a lot of people outside and they all want you to be safe. You understand that? They said I could come in and bring you out.

PLATO. Why?

JIM. They like you. [*Takes step toward him.*] Okay?

PLATO [*hesitating briefly*]. Come on! [*He and* JIM *turn to go.*]

[JUDY *steps into the* C *area from* U R C *and joins them.* PLATO *jumps nervously and then relaxes a little as he recognizes her.*]

JUDY. Hi, Plato!

PLATO. Hi, Judy. I thought you left me. I thought you both left me.

JUDY. Jim didn't leave you and I didn't leave you. We were coming back.

PLATO. I know. Jim told me.

JIM. We've got to go out.

PLATO. I'll come with you. [*He,* JIM, *and* JUDY *move quickly out* L. *Lights go out.*]

[*The stage is in darkness for a moment, and then the area* D L *is lit softly, and* JUDY, PLATO, *and* JIM *appear from off* D L.]

PLATO [*nervously, glancing* R]. Who're all those people?

JIM. They're the people I was telling you about. They're our friends.

PLATO [*holding back*]. There are too many. They make me nervous.

JIM. It's all right, Plato.

PLATO. I shot at one of them.

JIM. But you didn't hurt anybody.

PLATO [*drawing back even farther*]. Those aren't my friends. Make them go away.

JIM [*stepping forward a step and calling*]. Ray! Will you tell those guys to move back? It's important. [*Turns back to* PLATO *and* JUDY. *Suddenly, a searchlight comes on from offstage* R, *illuminating all three of them.* PLATO *looks around terrified, frozen for a moment, and then suddenly bolts off into the darkness* U C.]

[*The lights* D R *come on, illuminating* RAY, POLICE OFFICERS, FATHER, MOTHER, MRS. DAVIS, *and any extras.* PLATO, *from extreme* U C, *where he is illuminated by the spotlight which has followed him, swings his gun around and points at* RAY, *the* POLICE OFFICERS, *and the crowd.* MRS. DAVIS *screams as* OFFICER ONE *kneels down, calmly steadies his aim, and shoots* PLATO. PLATO, *wearing Jim's distinctive jacket, clutches his*

*right shoulder with his left hand—staggers, steps backward,
and then takes his gun with his left hand, letting his right
arm hang loose. As he transfers the gun,* OFFICER ONE, *who
has lowered his gun reluctantly, brings his gun up again.*
JIM *rushes from the still lighted* D L *area in front of him.*]

JIM. Don't shoot! Please don't shoot him! [*Turns and screams
at* PLATO.] Wait!

OFFICER ONE. Get out of my way! I can't let a nut run around
shooting into a crowd. I tried to drop his gun. He's tough.
He'll shoot left-handed.

JIM. You can't just shoot him. [*Turns to* RAY.] Ray, talk to
this guy.

RAY [*grimly*]. Jim, he's got to give up that gun.

JIM. Let me talk to him again.

JUDY [*rushing over from* D C *area*]. No, Jim! [*Light* D L *dims
out slowly.*]

FATHER. Jim—you can't!

JIM. I can't let him get shot. Let me try, Ray.

RAY. No. You'll get killed. It's too dangerous!

JIM. Someone's got to. [*Turns and calls.*] Plato! [*Starts to walk
toward* PLATO, U C, *who slowly lifts his gun as he comes
near.*]

PLATO. Keep away from me.

JIM. I can't, Plato—I've got to help you.

PLATO [*almost hysterically*]. They shot me—they shot me!
They could have killed me. They're all after me!

JIM [*slowly approaching*]. I'm not.

PLATO. Then get back—get out of my way.

JIM [*still moving slowly*]. Plato, you're going to have to shoot
me first.

PLATO. I will.

JIM. No, you won't. [*Pauses in his walking.*] I'm your friend.
It doesn't matter how frightened you are, you *know* I'm your
friend, and friends don't hurt each other.

PLATO [*backing up a step, hysterically*]. Stand back, Jim!
You're not my friend.

JIM [*advancing another step*]. I am trying to help you. You've got to trust me and do what I say. You'll be all right.

PLATO. You're lying! [*Levels gun at him.*] If you come another step, I'll shoot!

JIM. I'm your friend. You won't.

PLATO. I did once and this time I won't miss. Stand back—don't you hear me?

JIM. If you want to shoot me, go ahead. Remember, Plato, I'm going to help. I'm your friend and you have to trust your friends. Why am I here if I'm not trying to help? [*As he says this he advances until he is right in front of gun's muzzle. He holds out his hand.*] Give me the gun, Plato. [*There is a long pause, and then* PLATO *hands gun to* JIM *and a half second later falls slowly to floor in a faint.* RAY *and* POLICE OFFICERS *move quickly* U C. JUDY *runs to* JIM'S *side.* JIM *stands* U C, *behind* PLATO, *and stares down at him for a half second, and then he crouches down over* PLATO.] Plato. Plato. Hey, jerkpot! [*Nothing happens.*]

RAY [*to* OFFICER TWO]. Get the doc—right away. [OFFICERS ONE *and* TWO *go out* D R. JIM *reaches out and touches* PLATO. *He turns to* JUDY *and speaks quietly.*]

JIM. He isn't hurt bad. He'll be all right. [MRS. DAVIS *has moved* U C *and is sobbing quietly.* MOTHER *and* FATHER *have moved* U C, *also.*]

FATHER [*to* JIM]. For a minute—earlier—that jacket—[*Indicates jacket on* PLATO.]—I thought——[*Breaks off.*] You couldn't help it, son. [*Kneels down beside* JIM *and reaches out gently, but firmly.*] You've done everything a man can do. [*Takes* JIM *by elbow and starts to bring him to his feet.* JIM *resists and twists his body away, remaining kneeling.*] Stand up, Jim. I'll stand up with you. Let me *try* to be as strong as you want me to be. [JIM *turns and looks at his father for the first time. There is a long pause. Finally,* JIM *rises to his feet.* FATHER *rises with him.*]

[OFFICER ONE *and* OFFICER TWO *appear* D R *with a stretcher, which they set in front of* PLATO.]

JIM [*looking down at* PLATO]. He trusted me.

FATHER. And you can depend on me, son. Trust me. Whatever comes, we'll face it together, I swear. [JIM *puts his arm around his* FATHER'S *shoulder.* FATHER *looks at him and then puts his arm around* JIM'S *shoulder.* MOTHER *comes and stands beside them.* POLICE OFFICERS *stand aside as* MRS. DAVIS *kneels by* PLATO.]

MRS. DAVIS [*sobbing*]. This poor baby got nobody. Just *nobody*.

JIM. Sure he has. He's got us—he's got all of us. [POLICE OF-FICERS *start to put* PLATO *on stretcher. As they get ready to pick it up,* JIM *steps forward, puts blanket from stretcher over* PLATO. *The light* D R *fades out, leaving only* C *area still lit by searchlight.*]

PLATO [*weakly raising his hand and touching* JIM'S *hand*]. Thanks, Jim.

JIM. For the blanket?

PLATO. For everything.

JIM. Jerkpot.

RAY [*helping* MRS. DAVIS *to her feet*]. I'm sorry he got hurt but it isn't a serious wound. He fainted from loss of blood. He'll be all right.

MRS. DAVIS. My poor boy. He needs help—he needs help bad.

RAY. He's got a pretty good friend. [*Nods toward* JIM.] And for the rest—I'll see that he gets help—real help. Come with me. [*Puts an arm around her shoulder, and as she sobs he leads her out* D R. POLICE OFFICERS *take stretcher out* D R.]

JIM [*to his parents*]. There's something else that's important. [*Puts his arm around* JUDY, *who looks up at him. Then he continues.*] Mom, Dad—this is my friend. Her name is Judy. [*Searchlight goes out quickly. Stage is in darkness.*]

CURTAIN

PRODUCTION NOTES

The play is staged in three areas. Right, center and left. If the stage is narrow, these may be compressed into a smaller area by having the playing areas down right, up center and down left. In several of the scenes that are staged in the center area, it may be practical to increase the lighted area to include the whole stage for the duration of these brief scenes. The scenes best so treated are the planetarium scenes, the "chicken run" scene and the final scene.

The tire chain can be made from balsa wood or plastic dipped in aluminum paint. For the shots that are fired onstage, it is suggested that a "starter" pistol be used like those used for starting races at track meets.

Quickness of scene change is extremely desirable and a well trained crew who practice pushing on and off stage the few odd pieces of furniture that are used in the show will materially heighten the dramatic impact of the play.

A special sound effects record is available incorporating all the police sirens, "chicken run" automobile effects and major sound effects required in this play.